Studying Suzuki Piano:

More than Music

Senzay

Carole L. Bigler   *and*   **_Valery Lloyd-Watts_**

Carole Lindemann Bigler was born in Kingston, Pennsylvania. Her father, born in Germany and educated as a violinist and conductor, created a rich musical environment and provided her with lessons on piano at age four and pipe organ at fifteen.

She graduated Magna Cum Laude from Syracuse University, Syracuse, NY, with a major in piano and a minor in organ. In addition to tuition scholarships she received the Presser Music Award. Her teachers included Sydney Sukoenig, George Pappa-Stavrou, Ernst Bacon, Will O. Headlee, and Arthur Poister.

She taught music in the New York state school system and did graduate work at Ithaca College and at Cornell University where she studied pipe organ with Donald R. M. Patterson. She is organist for the First Congregational Church in Corning, NY, and has appeared in professional concert on both organ and piano.

Her involvement with the Suzuki approach to education began in 1967 when her son began violin study with Lorraine Fink through the Ithaca Talent Education program. She is a popular lecturer and teacher at Suzuki piano workshops and institutes. Since 1974 she has collaborated with Mrs. Lloyd-Watts in the presentation of teacher-training courses.

Mrs. Bigler is a resident of Big Flats, NY, in the Finger Lakes region. She is married and has two children.

Valery Lloyd-Watts, who began playing piano at age four, made her orchestral debut at twelve and became a scholarship student at the Royal Conservatory in Toronto and the Royal College of Music in London, England. She earned the Licentiate at the Royal Academy of Music and the Master of Music degree at the University of Wisconsin.

At nineteen she was invited by the BBC to give the premiere of the Fricker *Toccata for Piano and Orchestra* with the Liverpool Philharmonic Orchestra under John Pritchard. On the CBC she has been a soloist across Canada, and has also soloed with the McGill Chamber Orchestra, for WHA-TV in Madison, Wisconsin, and for the Programme of Arts and Culture for the International Olympics held in Canada in 1976.

Mrs. Lloyd-Watts also gives children's concerts, often in connection with Suzuki Talent Education workshops. She has been applying the principles of Suzuki's early music education to piano since 1971. Her introduction to the Suzuki philosophy came through Margery Aber, Director of the American Suzuki Institute at Stevens Point, WI, when her daughter began violin studies in 1967 and she observed a week-long workshop by Dr. Suzuki in Madison.

The entire Suzuki Piano School repertoire has been recorded by Mrs. Lloyd-Watts on five stereo discs for Senzay Edition Records of Ability Development Associates, Inc., Athens, Ohio. Now a resident of Kingston, Ontario, Canada, she is married and has two children.

Studying Suzuki Piano:

More than Music

A Handbook for Teachers, Parents, and Students

by Carole L. Bigler and Valery Lloyd-Watts

 A Senzay Edition

by Ability Development Associates, Inc.
subsidiary of Accura Music
Athens, Ohio, U.S.A.

ISBN: 0-918194-06-7
Library of Congress Catalog Card Number: LC 78-73088
Cover Design: Paul Bradford
Lithographed in the United States of America by Edwards Bros., Inc., Ann Arbor, Michigan.

Dedication

We would like to dedicate this book to all parents and teachers who, by cherishing children, help them to become independent and to fulfill their potential as fine human beings.

Clarification

Because the English language lacks a singular pronoun which can refer to either "he" or "she," for the sake of clarity and consistency, we have used, throughout the book, "he" to mean the student and "she," the teacher.

Acknowledgements

Many people have inspired and encouraged us in our endeavor to apply Dr. Suzuki's principles to our lives and to piano teaching.

We are especially grateful to:

Dr. Shinichi Suzuki whose ideas and loving spirit have provided the basis of our work.

Our Suzuki colleagues whose enthusiasm and dedication have inspired us and whose ideas have enhanced our teaching.

Constance Starr who initially introduced Suzuki piano to North America.

Haruko Kataoka who came so often from Japan and whose fine teaching exemplified and clarified the concept of Talent Education as it applies to the piano.

Margery Aber, Director of the American Suzuki Institute; Elaine Edwards, Director of the Emporia State University Suzuki Program; and Sanford Reuning, Director of the American Suzuki Institute-Northeast who gave us opportunities to present our material in teacher training courses.

All of our students who provided us with our teaching experiences, challenges, and victories.

Our students' parents who so willingly and lovingly shared their children and their ideas, joys, and problems with us.

Summy-Birchard Company for allowing us to reproduce copious excerpts from The Suzuki Method ™ *Suzuki Piano School* volumes.

Our publisher, Reginald H. Fink, who continuously helped us with his faith and optimism.

Our husbands Don and Bill and our children, Lloyd and Megan, Jeffrey and Pamela, whose unstinting love freed our minds and time for this project.

Table of Contents

Pedagogical Analysis of Volumes One through Six
of
The Suzuki Piano School

Table of Illustrations

PREFACE

Many piano teachers and parents have expressed a need for help in applying the principles of Dr. Shinichi Suzuki's philosophy of early music education. This book attempts to fill that need.

Beginning in 1976, we have been invited to present teacher-training courses in Suzuki piano pedagogy at Institutes in the U.S. and Canada. In these courses, we have tried to interpret faithfully Dr. Suzuki's principles and ideals, organizing them into a set of practical procedures for the piano teacher. Since the opportunities for Suzuki piano teacher-training in North America are still limited, it was suggested that we prepare our course in book form, to act as a reference for those who have taken our course and as a text for those who wish to learn about Suzuki piano.

In addition to a discussion of the Suzuki philosophy and a chapter each on motivating parents and students, we have included three chapters on preparing to be a Suzuki piano teacher, what to do at the first lessons, and how to structure an effective lesson. Since note-reading is an essential part of every musician's training, we have included the program we are finding very effective. The chapter on technique describes the scale program we use with our students: this program develops a secure understanding and mastery of scales and develops a positive rhythmic sense in the students. The chapters analysing the six Volumes of the Suzuki repertoire identify preview sections (the "hard parts"!) and discuss the musical and technical points of each piece: this has been done to help teachers who are suddenly faced with the enormous task of assimilating all of the Suzuki material and to help parents better understand the teacher's goals.

It is our intention that this book be used as an adjunct to attending workshops and Institutes. There is no substitute for observing Dr. Suzuki, Mrs. Haruko Kataoka, and other dedicated and fine teachers who interpret Dr. Suzuki's philosophy.

It is our hope that this book will help teachers, parents and students grow in an understanding of and appreciation for the philosophy of Dr. Shinichi Suzuki.

Carole L. Bigler and
Valery Lloyd-Watts, Jan. 1979.

Chapter 1
The Suzuki Philosophy

Introduction

Talent Education

Talent Education, the teaching method developed by Shinichi Suzuki, has grown to a world-wide movement and has revolutionized theories of education. Suzuki began this work in 1945 and still teaches with undiminished vitality, inspiring teachers and students with his dedication and humility.

Dr. Suzuki was born into the family of a violin manufacturer in Japan in 1898. He began playing the violin as a young adult. After only a few years of study in Japan, he traveled to Germany to further his violin studies with Karl Klingler. It was in Germany that he was exposed to great European musicians; he was also strongly influenced by Western culture. During this time he met his wife, Waltraud.

Suzuki brought European music to Japan on his return from Germany. He spent several years teaching by the traditional methods. The first seeds of what was to become the Talent Education Method came to him when he was asked to teach a four-year-old boy. As he searched for a way to teach such a young child, Suzuki had an inspiration about applying the way children learn to speak their language to music education.

Suzuki analyzed and developed his ideas over the next few years, but his work was interrupted by World War II. After the war he was invited to teach violin at a school near Matsumoto. He accepted with the condition that he be allowed to put his ideas into practice, in order to bring joy to the lives of all children. He knew, after the devastation of the war, that his life's work would be to do this by expanding their abilities through playing the violin.

Mother Tongue

Dr. Shinichi Suzuki's method of education is based on a single idea—he calls this idea mother tongue. Dr. Suzuki observed that all children learn to speak their own languages (mother tongues) with great accuracy, complete with local inflections. This he believes demonstrates a remarkable ability. Children are surrounded by these language sounds from birth, and he reasoned that if the children were surrounded by musical sounds to the same degree, they would develop an equally remarkable ability in music. This is the concept of mother tongue.

1

Dr. Suzuki's idea is not merely a method of education, but is more significantly a philosophy based on respect for the child as an individual and on the belief that ability is learned and not inherited. Because he believes that ability is talent and because he believes that all children can be well educated, he calls his method Talent Education.

Implications of the Mother Tongue Idea

1. No Failures
2. Environment Educates Children
3. Rate of Progress Is Dictated by the Child
4. Ability Breeds Ability
5. Happy Environment Yields High Standards, Great Ability

No Failures

The first and most potent implication of the mother tongue idea is that there are *no failures*. Any child who can speak his native language has the potential to learn to play the piano. Children who cannot learn as rapidly as others are often classified as slow or incapable, but Dr. Suzuki asks, "What child refuses to speak his or her native language?" If a child does not learn, it does not mean lack of ability, but rather that the teaching methods are not compatible with his present development or that the child has not been properly or sufficiently stimulated.

Environment Educates Children

The idea of mother tongue also implies that *environment and not heredity educates children*. An infant cannot speak, but has the ability to learn to speak. He can learn language, music, or anything that is stimulated by the environment. This is demonstrated by the fact that most Japanese children speak Japanese with ease, and most North American children speak English with ease. The environment determines the language.

Ability develops because of the environment. A child from a home where good English is spoken speaks good English; if the child comes from a family which uses poor English, he will speak poor English, too. A child can learn only that which his particular environment offers.

Dr. Suzuki said, "If we speak to a child only in the morning and in the evening, he will say only 'Good Morning' and 'Good Evening'!" A child who never hears good music will never be able to reproduce it. Children can be taught to make good music.

Rate of Progress Is Dictated by the Child

The third implication of the mother tongue idea is that *the rate of progress is dictated by the child* and not by age or by other standards. A child will walk only when he is ready and cannot be forced to walk earlier. Most parents are willing to accept this. They cannot however accept a child's not knowing the alphabet by the end of the first grade. They make the mistake of equating reading progress with chronological age. In the Suzuki philosophy, no child is compared to others of comparable age—the rate of progress is dictated by the child.

Ability Breeds Ability

The fourth implication is that *ability breeds more ability*. Children first learn to speak with simple words, and this ability leads to speaking complete sentences, followed by reading and writing. The accumulation of abilities results in accomplishment. In music, a child begins with simple skills, and develops and accumulates them. The final result is an accomplished musician.

Happy Environment Yields High Standards, Great Ability

Finally, the mother tongue approach implies that *children can have high standards and develop great ability in a happy environment*. All children develop the ability to speak fluently and greatly enjoy the process. It is commonly though mistakenly thought that great ability is gained through oppressively hard work.

Our society often wrongly equates work with drudgery. Work is food for the soul if the attitude towards it is positive. It is only through constructive effort that one is led to accomplishment and a sense of worth. The happiness of achieving a goal should not be greater than the joy of working towards it. A child repeats language sounds over and over until they are mastered. A positive parental response made the learning of this language ability pleasurable. This positive response is one of the keys to mother tongue learning and is one of the most significant educational contributions of Talent Education.

Procedures—How the Mother Tongue Method Works

1. Environment
   a. Parents
   b. Teacher

2. Emphasis on Repetition
3. Natural Progress
4. Enjoying the Mastery of Each Step
5. Attitude of the Parents

Environment—Parents

The key factor in the success of the mother tongue approach to education is *the environment*. The greatest influence in a child's environment comes from the parents, who have the major responsibility of providing security for their offspring. This security means providing food, shelter, and education, but most important of all, abundant love. If the parents demonstrate love and focus it on their child's efforts and accomplishments, learning, of music or any other subject, will be a happy experience. In Talent Education, the parents have the important role of providing good examples (music for the child to hear) and incentives to learn. These incentives are simply showing pleasure through rewards (praise, encouragement, and sometimes physical demonstrations)—the same kinds of responses parents have when their children first learn to speak. Parents can and should enjoy this time of musical discovery and learning with their child just as much as they delighted in the child's first words.

Environment—Teacher

The teacher is part of the learning environment and must have an attitude of love, support, and encouragement for the child. Suzuki education may be regarded as a triangle, the strongest structure found in nature. The parent and teacher represent two sides, giving strong support to the third side, the child. The three sides supporting each other provide the strongest foundation for learning.

Emphasis on Repetition

The second precept of Talent Education is the *emphasis on repetition*. Children listen to the recordings of their music over and over again and play their assignments many times. The number of repetitions required by a child during the learning process is unknown. We do not count how often we say "Mama" before the child actually learns the word. We are willing to repeat it as often as necessary. This attitude toward repetition is seldom found in our public schools. All of us remember teachers who said, "I've repeated that three times; you should have it by now!" Some children may have needed four repetitions, and others 40. The teachers and parents of Suzuki students are willing to provide opportunity and incentive for as many repetitions as the child needs.

Natural Progress

Thirdly, the mother tongue approach allows for a *natural progress through daily practice*. All abilities develop or improve with practice. A child speaks only simple words at first. Through daily practice, vocabulary grows. Athletes do not begin to condition themselves just a few days before a competition, but spend years gradually building up their strength and stamina. If they did not use the required muscles daily, they would not be able to reach their ultimate goal. Playing the piano must develop in the same way, moving one step at a time toward great accomplishment.

Enjoying the Mastery of Each Step

This natural progress allows time for *the child to enjoy mastering each step in the learning process*. The learning process proceeds without strain and pressure through consistent reinforcement. If a child is enjoying the success of his current ability and is progressing in small steady steps, future tasks will be of no concern. A child speaking his first words is not concerned about diagraming a sentence, but is simply enjoying the thrill of discovery and success.

Attitude of the Parents

Mother tongue education is successful because the *children are highly motivated by the everyday attitude of their parents*—sincere praise and encouragement reinforced by love. Our positive reaction to a child's first words motivates attempts at new words, just as our positive attitude toward piano playing will motivate attempts at new skills. Parents do not criticize or judge when their children are babies and neither should they when their children are older. When a child fails after attempting those first steps, we do not criticize. We praise the effort and offer help. We should never expect too much from a child, but we should appreciate every step in the learning process no matter how small it seems. If we pressure or criticize, we teach the child to resist or withdraw, but if we offer support, we give an opportunity to grow.

Other Benefits of Mother Tongue Education

1. Begins Learning at an Early Age
2. Develops Concentration
3. Develops the Ability to Memorize
4. Develops Coordination
5. Develops Sensitivity to Patterns
6. Develops Sensitivity to Beauty
7. Promotes a More Harmonious Family Life

8. Eliminates Friction and Tension Which Impede Learning
9. Promotes Self-Esteem

Begins Learning at an Early Age

In addition to learning to play an instrument, many other benefits are gained from Talent Education. Because children learn music in the same manner in which they learn to talk, Dr. Suzuki says their musical education can and should begin at birth. *Children can begin at an earlier age* than believed practical by traditional educators. This early start helps them to achieve a high ability at an age when they were traditionally thought to be just ready to begin. As a result of this early start, by the time they are older and have many more time conflicts, they are playing so well and feeling such success that they do not want to give up their music for other activities. Younger children also have more time for listening and practicing.

Develops Concentration

The mother tongue approach to education *helps to develop concentration*. At first, the pieces are short because the attention span is short, but as the student advances, the length of the pieces increases and concentration is extended. It is not unusual to see a five-year-old Suzuki student concentrate on a piece of music for as long as 15 minutes. The philosophy for practicing also builds the ability to concentrate. As the child's playing ability develops, practicing time increases. This is different from the traditional attitude of requiring 30 minutes at the piano every day. Half an hour may be far too long for a very young child and too little for an advanced student.

Develops the Ability to Memorize

One of the most exciting benefits of this program is *the development of the ability to memorize easily*. In traditional study, students memorize only on occasion so that memory becomes a problem rather than an asset, and a memory slip is the dread of all. In Talent Education, memory is a part of the every-day work. Because it is reinforced every day, it is not dreaded. Just as we are not afraid of forgetting words when talking, the Suzuki student is not afraid of forgetting notes when playing.

At the beginning of study, the student memorizes short pieces, but retains each one in his repertoire. Gradually the pieces become longer, and since the previous pieces are retained, the memory is constantly exercised and trained. Amazingly, because the development is gradual and steady, a student can memorize a three-movement sonata just as easily as he memorized a four-phase folk song. This memory development carries over quite readily into other areas of learning. Because the child has developed the memorizing ability and along with it an ability to organize his thinking, memory work in school improves. One third grade student who was Suzuki-trained from age three was able to memorize the six-times table in just one evening. To this child the memorization was not something to fear, but simply a task which required a little time. How wonderful it would be if all children could approach multiplication tables with such confidence and ease!

Develops Coordination

Because playing the piano is a physical skill, the *child is developing coordination to a fine degree.* It requires the control of small muscles to play the piano, and while the child is learning this small-motor control, other coordinational skills become easier. Handwriting often improves as well as athletic ability.

Develops Sensitivity to Patterns

Suzuki students *develop an acute sensitivity to patterns,* not only in music, but also in speech, writing, and mathematics. To these students, learning which involves patterns is not a new experience, but simply an expansion of an ability the student has already developed.

Develops Sensitivity to Beauty

In addition to the sensitivity to patterns, the child *develops sensitivity to beauty.* This sensitivity is first awakened through music, but is easily extended to art, literature, nature, and most importantly, human qualities. A child who learns to be sensitive to the beauty in people will have developed a life-enhancing feeling even greater than the ability to create music. This sensitivity for humanity is a basic concern of Dr. Suzuki and a keystone of his philosophy.

Promotes a More Harmonious Family Life

The sensitivity the child develops and the loving spirit of the Suzuki approach *helps to promote a more harmonious family life.* Since parents are so directly involved with the child's musical education and are constantly reminded of the attitudes and actions that will help their children, families create a bond of common interest and effort that unites and strengthens them. Many parents readily admit that they have become more effective parents since they became involved with the Suzuki program, and have extended this effectiveness to their dealings with children who are not Suzuki students.

Eliminates Friction and Tension Which Impede Learning

The Suzuki philosophy is based on a loving spirit and positive attitudes which help to *eliminate the friction and tension which can impede the learning process.* Glen Doman in *How to Teach Your Baby to Read* states, "a child is the most sensitive instrument imaginable." A child who is exposed to beauty and who learns with high spirit can create and recreate beauty easily because there are no negative obstacles.

Promotes Self-Esteem

The Suzuki method of education *promotes self-esteem,* the most significant and worthwhile benefit of all. Whenever a person develops a new ability, human growth occurs. The development of ability creates

Photograph by Arthur Montzka

self-esteem. Liking oneself frees a person to like others. Liking oneself and liking others contributes to harmonious living and therefore creates a better world.

Creating an environment in which all children can realize their potential for happiness and superior ability is the essence of Shinichi Suzuki's philosophy.

Chapter 2

Preparing To Be a Suzuki Teacher

Introduction

Prior to the emergence of hundreds of highly skilled violinists (the products of Dr. Suzuki's philosophy and teaching procedures), it was believed that only a few gifted individuals could attain superior musicianship and performing ability. Now, it has been proven that all children can be helped to develop superior ability in music, given the combination of good teaching, loving support, and diligent, consistent effort.

Similarly, as a result of working with Dr. Suzuki's philosophy and of applying his teaching principles, we believe that *all teachers can develop superior teaching ability!* But what are the givens that must accompany such a forceful statement? The teacher must develop personal qualities compatible with Dr. Suzuki's philosophy, keyboard abilities and musicianship, and a systematic approach to teaching.

These three major areas require careful analysis in order to see the individual parts and how they combine to create a master teacher such as Shinichi Suzuki. It must be recognized that the process of becoming a master teacher is a lifelong undertaking. Dr. Suzuki has said, "When I am 90, then I will be a teacher but just now, I am learning how to teach!" It is a dynamic process of learning and growth that has as its goal the ability to communicate knowledge in such a way that the student can absorb all that the teacher has to offer and to go beyond that point independently to new insights and abilities.

Personal Qualities of a Suzuki Teacher

1. Love of Children
2. Love of Music
3. Enthusiasm
4. Personal Warmth
5. Self-Discipline
6. Sensitivity to Varied Personalities
7. Ability to Praise
8. Ability to Organize
9. Good Personal Practice Habits

Love of Children

The basic premise of Dr. Suzuki's philosophy is the love of and respect for each child as an individual. With this always foremost in our minds, we must treat the child as a valued person whose happiness, well-being, and musical development are of major importance to us. The title of Suzuki's book, *Nurtured by Love,* is significant. We are charged with the responsibility of nurturing the growth of the children's musical abilities as carefully as we would the growth of a slip of a rare and beautiful plant.

Love of Music

Most of us have become teachers because we love music. Those who do not should consider a different career for it is of the utmost importance to love what we teach.

Enthusiasm

Enthusiasm is really an expansion of love. If we love something, we speak of it in glowing terms. If we are not excited about music, how is it possible to generate excitement in the child? Enthusiasm is contagious!

Personal Warmth

Children are certainly quick to sense our feelings and if we are stiff or aloof in our manner, they may become tense. This is not to say that one must use pet names or express oneself in an uncomfortable or unnatural way. Warmth is an internal quality that reveals itself without a word or a conscious gesture to the person to whom we turn our attention. The means of expressing warmth are as unique and as varied as are people.

Self-Discipline

The challenge of learning all of the Suzuki repertoire requires a great deal of self-discipline. We must accept that responsibility, continuously striving to increase our understanding of the materials we are presenting.

It requires self-discipline to respond positively to a negative child. During a workshop, one five-year-old boy, when it was his turn, clutched his mother and refused to play. Without commenting on this, the teacher took a tennis ball from her purse and let it drop from the stage to the floor. Easily and calmly, she asked the child to retrieve the ball for her. When he did this willingly, the teacher then asked him to play catch with her. While they played, the teacher commented approvingly on how well the child caught and held the ball. Finally, she asked the child to show how well he could hold the ball over the keyboard. (When the ball is removed, the hand is in very good playing position. See Chapter 8—*The First Lessons.*) The child responded without hesitation, and he was soon proudly playing the *Twinkle Variations* all the way through hands together. By the time his lesson was over it was with the greatest reluctance that the child left the piano!

In addition to being able to deal positively with a negative child, teachers must be able to control their own moods and deal pleasantly with the children. Upsetting incidents occur without warning, but we adults must be able to control our thoughts and feelings, setting a positive example for the students.

Sensitivity to Varied Personalities

Each child is unique, requiring a specially tailored approach. This recognition of the child's uniqueness allows a teacher to present the *Twinkle Variations* thousands of times without ever feeling bored. It is a joy to watch a young person grasp a new concept successfully, quickly, and easily!

Among the personalities the teacher will meet and have to deal with are those of the parents. Motivating the parents requires energy and tact, as they often have strong opinions which may not be totally compatible with the new ideas being presented to them. (See Chapter 3—*Helping Parents Help Their Children.*)

Ability to Praise

One of the delights of observing Dr. Suzuki's teaching is listening to his comments to the children after they have played. His praise is always generous and appropriate. The breadth of his understanding and his positive approach makes children eager to try their best. He continually urges the teachers and parents to "praise, praise, praise," knowing that encouragement rather than criticism motivates a person. (See Chapter 4—*Motivating Students.*) Sometimes a teacher must search for something to praise in a generally poor performance. We often tell the parents, "Your child deserves praise for being at the instrument; that effort alone is worthy of recognition." Appropriateness of praise is important. One must not say "The tone was beautiful" if it was not. If the notes were correct, one could say, "All of the notes were correct, and this fine accomplishment can free you to listen for a beautiful tone as well." Dr. Haim Ginott in his book *Between Parent and Child* has a valuable chapter on helpful and unhelpful praise; it is recommended reading for teachers as well as parents.

Praising the parent is as important as praising the child because his or her role is essential to the child's success. Recognizing the parent's contributions during the lesson encourages cooperation during daily practice.

Praise can be used effectively to correct negative behavior. One lively five-year-old was distracting the other children in a large group class. The teacher, spotting the potential troublemaker, invited him to come onstage as her special helper to arrange the footstool for each child as he or she sat at the piano. (This drew attention to the child who was craving it—usually the motivation for most unattractive social behavior—and isolated him from the group in one stroke.) Periodically during the rest of the hour, the teacher praised her helper for the fine job he was doing, and at the conclusion of the class, had all of the children applaud him for his efforts.

Ability to Organize

Organization of personal as well as professional time is mandatory. Many teachers know that the busier they are, the more they can accomplish—if their day is planned. Lessons are usually more successful if they, too, are planned carefully. Each lesson, in order to be organized effectively, must be part of the overall plan for that student. (See "Setting Goals for Students" in this chapter and Chapter 5—*Structuring an Effective Lesson.*)

Good Personal Practice Habits

Daily practice helps to make the repertoire as familiar as one's own name, a goal that Dr. Suzuki considers desirable for all musicians. Striving for good tone and rhythm is important. Tape recording a practice session can be helpful if it is not intimidating or threatening. Listening to the playback can be enormously helpful in developing musical sensitivity if one listens with concentration for a specific detail each time (*e.g.,* phrasing, ornaments, tone, *etc.*). Listening in this manner is like being your own Suzuki teacher—concentrating on one step at a time. Praise yourself for the good things, also; it is just as important as praise for a student.

Keyboard Abilities and Musicianship

It is probably true that all of the present North American Suzuki piano teachers have had their musical training in a traditional, note-reading approach. None have had the opportunity to learn as Suzuki students, absorbing the music through the ears, one step at a time, over a period of years. Teachers, who see the exciting results and advantages of Suzuki teaching and who wish to teach this way, are suddenly faced with learning six volumes of literature thoroughly in order to teach it, step by step, to the students. This is a formidable task! The central purpose of this book is to make that task easier. At present, no comprehensive course is available for the teaching of Suzuki piano, and most teachers would be financially unable to take one or two years' leave in order to prepare themselves. The following suggestions are designed to help ease this task:

1. Listen to the recordings in the same way that the students are required to listen, daily and as frequently as possible.
2. Practice the repertoire.
3. Observe other teachers as much as possible.
4. Attend as many workshops as possible.

When practicing the repertoire, analyze each piece to discover every detail of phrasing, fingering, ornamentation, *legato,* staccato, *portato* touches, slurring effects, and the appropriate quality of sound needed for each note. This careful study and analysis will reveal the difficult parts (most likely to be used as *Preview Material,* see Chapters 9 through 14), the musical purpose, and the technical purpose.

What is a Step?

Each detail in the Suzuki approach is called a STEP. It is important to clarify just what is meant by a step since this is one of the cornerstones of Suzuki teaching.

A step is the smallest part of a musical passage that the child can grasp. This unit (step) helps him to execute a small segment of the music with technical accuracy. Mastering one step allows the student to add another step. The accumulation of several mastered single steps builds the complex ability required to play the piece. This building process is basic to all learning. Consider the impossible task of trying to teach addition to a child who cannot yet count.

The concept of adapting the size of the step to the child is one of Dr. Suzuki's great contributions to music education. It is this concept that makes it possible to introduce playing skills to very young children.

One of the teacher's prime responsibilities is learning to isolate the particular steps required by a particular student. Learning what a step is is a fascinating process of discovery, like Russian nested dolls—each step seems to have another step inside it, and the steps become smaller and clearer as the teacher absorbs, teaches, and reteaches the pieces. Elizabeth Mills in *The Suzuki Concept* says, "What I once thought was a single step I now realize was 20." In each small group of notes in a piece, different steps may be combined. For example the child may have to:

1. Remember the sequence of notes.
2. Make a change of hand position (*e.g., Clair de Lune,* third phrase).
3. Combine *legato* and staccato within a phrase (*e.g., Little Play- mates*).
4. Play several notes in the right hand and only one or two in the left hand (*e.g., Allegro,* first phrase).
5. Make the notes of one hand connect in sound while playing a detached or repeated note in the other hand (*e.g., Lightly Row,* first measure).

By knowing the steps and the ways in which they combine in the piece, the teacher is better able to help when the child experiences difficulty.

Dividing the learning process into steps is similar to learning how to program a computer in reverse. In programing a computer, one must tell it every single step to make; the computer will not make any decisions for itself, not even to look at the next card. A teacher presenting a piece of music to a child usually starts with a concept of the final result and must be able to divide the complexities of the music into units that a child can understand and then link together. The child's mind is more sophisticated than the most complex and elaborate machine; the child can, and will, make connections and extrapolations beyond the scope of the most complicated computer. The point is that in order to help most efficiently, the teacher must analyze all the possible steps that occur in playing music. Only by understanding what constitutes each step is it possible to spot accurately what is necessary for corrections.

No two children learn a piece in the same manner, nor with the same ease, and the teacher will probably have to use a combination of steps that is different for each child.

Mastery of the Step

Mastery of the step means the child can play that part (which may be as little as two notes) correctly and easily *every* time he plays it. Mastery must be at the 100 percent level. For some children, this mastery may take only a few repetitions, for others, many, many repetitions. It is very important for the parents to understand that the child be allowed as much time as he needs for mastery, since no one can predict how long, nor how many repetitions, will be needed.

STOP-PREPARE

Once a teacher understands what constitutes a step and how to isolate it, using the STOP-PREPARE technique guarantees that the child will successfully absorb and master the step. STOP-PREPARE is the single most valuable tool a Suzuki teacher has, one that will be indispensable in teaching the entire Suzuki repertoire. It is as important in teaching the Mozart *Sonata, K 331* in Volume 6 as it is in teaching of *Twinkle Variations.*

STOP-PREPARE describes two functions: physically STOP and mentally PREPARE. This may happen between any two consecutive steps. The child plays the first step that is already mastered (and STOPS at this point), then, while stopped, PREPARES his mind and fingers to play the next step. (This second step should have already been mastered as a single step.) Combining two mastered steps constitutes a new step and consequently creates a new ability.

The Advantages of STOP-PREPARE

Dr. Suzuki says STOP-PREPARE means that you are practicing fast, very slowly. Each of the steps must be played at the concert performance tempo of the totally perfected piece. The traditional learning process requires the child to learn the entire piece by playing it very *slowly* from beginning to end in order to gain a concept of the whole. In the Suzuki approach, by listening to the recordings, the child develops a concept of the whole long before he ever starts to learn the piece. (See also, "Importance of Listening" in Chapter 3—*Helping Parents to Help Their Children.*) Once the traditional student has laboriously gained a conception of the whole, the tempo is gradually increased to the ultimate goal. This method forces the child to learn 50 different pieces (different *tempi*) using the same notes! The Suzuki student learns one piece once!

When and How to Eliminate STOP-PREPARE

As soon as the child can grasp the manner in which the two steps link, he will almost automatically remove the long STOP-PREPARE, thus allowing the two steps to merge into one new, flowing, technically perfect step. This is possible because the child knows from listening what it should sound like without the STOP. Combining the steps is like building a puzzle; each little fragment is perfect, and when they are all joined, the picture is an integrated whole.

After carefully analyzing the pieces to determine the steps and the ways in which they combine, the teacher will find it relatively easy to implement the following two suggestions:

1. Learn to recognize the technical features of the more advanced repertoire which relate to and take advantage of the skills already

developed. (See the analysis of the volumes, Chapters 9 through 14 for suggestions.)

2. Create exercises which help solve specific technical problems. This skill develops best with experience in teaching and is one of the very rewarding aspects of Suzuki teaching—finding the means to help a student master difficulties.

Developing a Systematic Approach to Teaching

Being systematic does not restrict creativity. Some teachers reject the idea of teaching Suzuki piano because the repertoire is predetermined. This is like believing that creativity in English composition is limited because the alphabet is defined. The scope of teaching is vast, even when using these selected pieces. By using a common repertoire, the teacher presents the pieces with an everdeveloping skill. The student develops a greater awareness of the idiom by retaining each piece through constant practice and review and by hearing other students playing the same repertoire. A foundation of musicianship built on a thorough command of the Baroque and Classical eras gives the student a solid base from which to progress to Romantic, Impressionist, and Contemporary music. Young children learn best by imitation; older children and adults, by association. A student with a background in the Baroque and Classical repertoire has a basis for comparison and association.

Some teachers accept using the repertoire but reserve the right to change the order of presentation or omit some pieces altogether. An analysis of the pieces reveals that great care and skill have gone into the selection and progression of the repertoire. Each piece has a special musical or technical point (See Chapters 9 through 14) or, in the case of some of the easier pieces in the later volumes, is a reward after mastering an especially difficult task. When the teacher understands these goals, each piece becomes a treasure, and skipping any of them is a loss. It is possible to build the student's desire for each piece by discussing the special skills it involves some time before study actually begins. By allowing the child to master each step along the way, self-confidence is established and will create eagerness to try the new challenge.

A systematic approach to all aspects of teaching (the Suzuki repertoire, note-reading, technique, and review) is found in Chapter 5—*Structuring an Effective Lesson*. With the interconnecting systems in mind, the teacher is then equipped to set meaningful and realistic goals for the students.

Setting Goals for Students

Implicit in the systematic approach is a *long-term plan for each student*. Robert Mager in the preface to *Preparing Instructional Objectives* relates the following fable:

Once upon a time a Sea Horse gathered up his seven pieces-of-eight and cantered out to find his fortune. Before he had traveled very far he met an Eel, who said,
"Psst. Hey, bud. Where 'ya goin'?"

"I'm going out to find my fortune," replied the Sea Horse, proudly.

"You're in luck," said the Eel. "For four pieces-of-eight you can have this speedy flipper, and then you'll be able to get there a lot faster."

"Gee, that's swell," said the Sea Horse, and paid the money and put on the flipper and slithered off at twice his former speed. Soon he came upon a Sponge, who said, "Psst. Hey, bud. Where 'ya goin'?"

"I'm going out to find my fortune," replied the Sea Horse.

"You're in luck," said the Sponge. "For a small fee I will let you have this jet-propelled scooter so that you will be able to travel a lot faster."

So the Sea Horse bought the scooter with his remaining money and went zooming thru the sea five times as fast. Soon he came upon a Shark, who said,

"Psst. Hey, bud. Where 'ya goin'?"

"I'm going to find my fortune," replied the Sea Horse.

"You're in luck. If you'll take this short cut," said the Shark, pointing to his open mouth, "you'll save yourself a lot of time."

"Gee, thanks," said the Sea Horse, and zoomed off into the interior of the Shark, and was never heard from again.

The moral of this fable is that if you're not sure where you're going, you're liable to end up someplace else.[1]

A long-term plan is made up of a series of steps (smaller goals) designed to produce a predetermined result. Having the goal in mind eliminates the wasting of time and effort on unnecessary study. For example, it would be pointless to ask a student to memorize the entire Haydn *Sonata* in Volume 5 hands separately; in fact, it would be a detriment since many of the rhythmic problems can only be solved hands together. (See Chapter 13——*Studying Volume 5* for preview material.)

In preparing a long-term plan for the student, the teacher should not try to plan further ahead than one year. Goals should be realistic and concrete, and should reflect the teacher's concern for technical and musical growth. (*e.g.,* The teacher's goal for a child might be to learn and master the Bach *Minuets* at the end of Volume 4.) These goals are, for the most part, not communicated to the child, but are the teacher's private concern. The point is not to apply pressure to the child (if he or she did not meet the expectations, a sense of failure might result), but to provide the teacher with an overall plan. Once the teacher has defined the long-term goal, the short-term goals will be easier to define. For example, playing an entire piece without error may be the short-term goal for a young student. Short-term goals may span a few weeks or a semester. From the short-term goal, comes the emphasis for the weekly lesson. With precise goals, each lesson will have greater coherence and impact for the student.

Considering the Attributes of the Child

The attributes of each child must be considered when the teacher plans the goals. Some children have excellent coordination but have

---

[1] Robert Mager. *Preparing Instructional Objectives.* Palo Alto, Calif.: Fearon Publishers, 1962, 1975. Preface. Reprinted by permission.

parents who do not read music. So the teacher may have to spend a few minutes of each lesson making sure that the parents understand the objectives of that particular lesson. One child may be less well coordinated but have a highly supportive parent. Often these students do extremely well since a very large factor in the success of the program is the support the child receives at home. Another intelligent, coordinated child may have a parent with a negative attitude. This is usually a very difficult situation, and the teacher may have to spend a great deal of time and energy creating a positive attitude in a parent towards the child and the child's efforts. Ideally, of course, there is a coordinated, eager, sensitive child who has a happy, supportive, and conscientious parent. Every means at the teacher's disposal must be used to help the parents create a good environment for the child and his education no matter what physical or mental attributes the child exhibits initially. Dr. Suzuki has shown by his example that seemingly miraculous results can occur as a result of careful analysis and nurturing of a child's abilities. The most important goal we can have as teachers is to help the child increase self-esteem by increasing abilities.

Conclusion: Applying the Suzuki Philosophy in the North American Culture

The North American educational philosophy is, by and large, based on competition. "Let the best man win." "Winning isn't everything, it's the *only* thing!" Such sayings are a common part of our everyday experience. Schools are based mostly on testing and peer grading (a system which compares one student to another rather than to an objective grading system). The only appropriate competition should be to compete with one's own potential. What ability has the child developed today that was not there yesterday? What grasp of a concept is now fully owned that was only vaguely understood before? These are the only concerns the students should have. All other competitiveness should be avoided, particularly in Suzuki study. Students must be encouraged to rejoice in the efforts of their fellow students and to know that with time and consistent effort their work will develop also. When, not if, is the point. Dr. Wayne W. Dyer in *Your Erroneous Zones* states,

> Aptitude is really a function of time rather than some inborn quality. One support for this belief can be found in the grade norms for standardized achievement tests. These norms demonstrate that scores achieved by the top students at one grade level are achieved by the majority of students at a later grade level. Further studies show that although most students eventually reach mastery on each learning task, some students achieve mastery much sooner than do others. Yet the label 'deficient' or even 'retarded' is often attached to those who move more slowly toward absolute mastery of a skill.[2]

A teacher must take particular care not to compare one student to another; otherwise competition for approval develops among the

---

[2]Wayne W. Dyer, *Your Erroneous Zones* (New York: Funk & Wagnalls, 1976), p. 36–37. Reprinted by permission.

students. Teachers, without consciously meaning to, can encourage competition between themselves and other teachers. This usually takes the form of what we call the *Progress Trap:* "X's students have studied only one year and can already play all of Volume 2 brilliantly. Mine aren't doing that well. What am I doing wrong? She must be a better teacher than I am!" Also, parents and other teachers may ask, "How long have you been teaching? What is your most advanced student playing? Did you hear X's student who is only four and can play all six volumes perfectly?" These questions should not be allowed to intimidate any sincere teacher. With time, desire, and effort, both teacher and student will achieve their goals. In the meantime, rejoice in the knowledge that the students are receiving a joyous introduction to music that they probably wouldn't have had otherwise. Be happy for the growth in their self-esteem, and remember that "high spirit is more important than high fame." (Dr. Suzuki) This applies to teachers too! If the students are developing confidence, they will be striving to develop and improve their abilities. With the development of these feelings, they are taking a measure of responsibility for their own actions.

We respect and admire all of our Suzuki colleagues. By striving to develop the qualities they respect and admire in Dr. Suzuki, by striving to improve their own abilities, they develop a spirit of joy and sincerity that is inspiring to all who know them. Their teaching success is bred by their efforts to learn and their desire to teach. Kenneth Clark in his autobiography *Another Part of the Wood* says: "Education involves a balance of effort and delight." The combination of this effort and delight makes Suzuki teaching the adventure of a lifetime!

Chapter 3
Helping Parents Help Their Children

Introduction

The ability to create a great work of art is limited to a few individuals; however, creation of a noble spirit in a human being is possible for *all* parents. Fulfilling this possibility is a long and complex process requiring love, high ideals, understanding of the growth process, and a willingness to allow the child to mature according to his own inner timetable. Parents sensitive to these facets of human development can create an environment in which the child, nurtured by love, can reach the full potential of physical, mental, and emotional growth.

The Role of the Parents in the Education of Their Children

The Joys

The role parents play in the education of their children is of major and critical importance. Gilbert Highet states, "the relation between parents and children is essentially based on teaching," and parents should be made aware of the joys as well as the responsibilities of this relationship.

The joys are to be found in watching the child become a happier person who learns to set goals and achieve them, in seeing his development in the acquisition of a difficult and complex skill, and in hearing the child recreate music composed by some of the greatest minds of all ages. Dr. Suzuki states in *Nurtured by Love* that by being exposed to the music of these noble beings, and by constantly striving to express the musical ideals, the child will be similarly inspired and ennobled. "Bach, Mozart, Beethoven—without exception they live clearly and palpably in their music and speak forcefully to us, purifying us, refining us and awakening in us the highest joy and emotion."

The Responsibilities

The responsibility for teaching children, in a Suzuki program, has two distinct parts: The child must be helped to develop an ear for music, and each step in the learning process must be mastered. Helping the child achieve these goals is the responsibility of the parents. Helping the parents help their child is the responsibility of the teacher who must act as interpreter of the philosophy, as the source of inspiration to the child, and as guide for the parents. By following the teacher's instructions faithfully during the week, the parents will be able to help their child most effectively.

The Key to Success

Parents are the key to the success of a Suzuki program because of the large role they have to play. It is important that the teacher, at the outset of their involvement, advise them carefully and honestly of the commitment they are making. We suggest that a teacher interview prospective parents and if the teacher believes that the parents' time for this commitment is limited, the teacher should spend more time discussing the philosophy and responsibilities with them before the child begins any lessons. In the long view, this is the kindest thing for the child, since only with the support of the parents will he make good and happy progress. Being a Suzuki parent is time-consuming, and we must be sure the parents understand that their help and attention is required until the child gains the maturity and proficiency which allow independent work.

The Role of the Teacher in the Guidance of the Parents

Education

The teacher is responsible for the education and encouragement of the parents. The role that music can play in the life of the child and the family must be explained. The parents must be told and shown by example how they can best help the child.

In educating the parents, the teacher must make sure they understand that the aim of all education should be the ultimate independence of the child. Education should provide the skills and knowledge to direct one's own learning and future pursuits. Piano study should be considered a segment of a child's total education just as mathematics, language, and science contribute to the breadth of a well-educated person. We do not expect the child to be a concert pianist, a mathematician, and a scientist simultaneously. However, should the student decide as a young adult to make a career as a concert pianist, he will have a good foundation on which to build. The main purpose of this approach to the piano and the common goal of both parents and teacher, is the enrichment of the life of the child.

Encouragement

The teacher must constantly *encourage the parents*. This encouragement is as important to the parents as it is to the child. The teacher must be sure to praise the parents' efforts and let them know they are appreciated. They must understand the Suzuki philosophy and procedures. The combination of the teacher's recognition and the parents' knowledge will create a strong support for the child.

Educating the Parents

We believe that the Suzuki teacher is responsible for educating the parents in the following three areas:

1. The Suzuki Philosophy.
2. Helping the Child Develop an Ear for Music.
3. Practicing Effectively with Their Child.

The Suzuki Philosophy

The first and most essential task, *educating the parents in the Suzuki philosophy*, is largely accomplished by having the parents own and read Dr. Suzuki's *Nurtured by Love*. It must be readily available for reference and inspiration because its contents are so potent that they cannot possibly be absorbed and digested in one reading.

Helping the Child Develop an Ear for Music

The second task, *teaching the parents how to help the child develop an ear for music,* involves the use of recordings. In the Suzuki program the child listens repeatedly to the music he is going to learn. It is essential that the recorded performance of the music be of the highest quality, technically and musically, so that the child will have an ideal model. Recordings have been made of all of the volumes of the Suzuki repertoire and the parents are asked, as their prime contribution to the education of their child in the Suzuki program, that the recordings be played in the presence of the child as much as possible. It is not necessary for the child to sit and listen exclusively. Playing, reading, or any of a wide variety of activities is permissible. Dr. Suzuki says that the child does not even need to be in the same room with the music! As long as it is audible, the child will be absorbing many things from the music.

The Importance of Listening   *The importance of listening to the recordings must be stressed again and again.* The whole basis of Suzuki education is imitation and repetition. If a child does not hear the recordings enough, learning will be made difficult, if not impossible. In the beginning, parents are generally conscientious about this, but as time passes they often neglect the records and consequently wonder why the child is having difficulty. One parent commented that her child could learn *London Bridge* much more easily than *French Children's Song*. The problem was not the child, but the parent. The child was not hearing the record enough. *London Bridge* had already been a familiar song to the child. It was the parent's responsibility to make sure that *French Children's Song* was just as familiar. Dr. Suzuki stresses that listening to the recordings is twice as important as practicing.

Parents need to understand that listening to the recordings teaches many things, such as:

a. Note Sequences.
b. Pattern Recognition.
c. Pitch Sensitivity.
d. Memory.

e. New Sequence Memorization.
f. Sensitivity to Musical Expression.

NOTE SEQUENCES   *Learning the sequence of notes* is important but is only one of the benefits of constant listening.

PATTERN RECOGNITION   From the earliest piece, *Twinkle Variations,* the students are taught to recognize *recurring patterns* (the peanut butter and jelly sandwich simile (See Chapter 9—*Studying Volume 1*) is more than just a memory aid). This understanding of patterns is the first step in the development of a concept of musical forms.

PITCH SENSITIVITY   *Sensitivity to pitch* develops for piano students just as acutely as it does for violin students. Since the pianist has no control over the pitch, this sensitivity is not stressed as much; however, it is an advantage to all musicians. Children love to pick out pieces that are coming later in their repertoire and they usually experiment until they are matching the pitch to the recording.

MEMORY   Every piece that the student learns is thoroughly memorized; every piece becomes a part of the musical vocabulary and is not forgotten, just as we do not forget words in our speaking vocabulary. Because of this concept, students are able to *recall the pieces accurately* for a very long time. This ability improves as the listening experience accumulates and some students can recall with 100 percent accuracy pieces they learned several years earlier.

NEW SEQUENCE MEMORIZATION   Suzuki students, because of their great sensitivity to patterns, become adept at memorizing whole sequences quickly. They consequently become better sight-readers. For example, a Suzuki student sight-reading Kabalevsky's *A Little Joke* will, by the end of four measures, have recognized and will correctly execute the recurring pattern which is the basis of the piece and the joke.

SENSITIVITY TO MUSICAL EXPRESSION   The greatest of all the benefits of the constant exposure to the recordings is the child's increasing sensitivity to musical expression. As familiarity with the music grows, the child becomes enormously sensitive to the nuances of musical expression. In no way does the child copy the interpretation of the recording. Because of a solid understanding of the music, the child becomes free to express his own musical ideas.

Practicing Effectively with Their Child

The third task, explaining to the parents *how to practice effectively with their child,* is complex. The easiest way to simplify this task is to teach the parents each step in the learning process. Clarifying the steps for the parents requires a thorough mastery of the repertoire on the part of the teacher.

The Roles of the Parent and Other Relatives

Once the parents have a basic understanding of the Suzuki approach and procedures to education, the teacher can then discuss the following:

1. The Role of the Parent at the Lesson.

2. The Role of the Parent at Home.
3. The Role of Other Relatives at Home.

The Role of the Parent at the Lesson

The parent should sit close enough to the piano to observe everything as it happens at the lesson. The lesson provides a model to follow when the child practices during the week. The more thoroughly the parent understands what is happening, the better he or she can help the child at home. Having a notebook in which to write the assignments and to make notes about special things, (*e.g.,* how well the child played a particular piece), is a good idea. It is important for the child to be reminded of accomplishments in addition to being reminded of the areas in which improvement is needed. The parent should also hold the music in order to be able to mark fingerings, dynamics, slurring, staccato, *etc.,* and most importantly, where STOP-PREPARE occurs. (This is discussed fully in Chapter 2—*Preparing To Be a Suzuki Teacher.*)

Because the full attention of the parent is needed, it is important that there be no distractions during the lesson. We usually request that siblings come to the lessons only if they can amuse themselves quietly while the lesson is in progress. Being attentive during the lesson gives the parent the opportunity to learn what the victories[3] are so they can be recognized during the week. Spotting those victories can and should be one of the most exciting happenings in the practice session.

The role of the parent is really that of an interested observer rather than a participant. It is important to make this distinction because some keen parents innocently interject so much that the flow of the lesson between the teacher and child is interrupted. The parent must be willing to allow the teacher to handle the child in all situations *unless the teacher requests help.* One very bright child, who liked to talk, always made interesting but unusual connections between the lesson subject and other topics in her mind. Once she had said her piece, and this sometimes took quite a while, she was very willing to continue working diligently at the lesson. To the benefit of the teacher, the mother, instead of remonstrating with her daughter, sat quietly, and let the teacher bring the child back to concentration in her own way.

Paradoxically, in spite of playing the role of an interested silent observer, the parent must be able to stop the lesson if there is a point or an assignment he or she does not understand. There must be no doubt in the parent's mind as to a) the assignment, and b) the goal, and the teacher must be willing to clarify it. A parent should not engage the teacher in irrelevant social conversation; the child, for whom the lesson time is meant, should not be kept waiting.

---

[3]A victory occurs when a child demonstrates the ability to do a single step that formerly he could not do. A psychologist defines learning as a change in behavior. Thus a change in behavior (doing something that could not or would not be done previously) is learning and learning is a victory.

The Role of the Parent at Home

Dr. Suzuki says "Praise, praise, praise." Rewards to children are very important, and our praise is probably the most valuable motivational tool we have. A parent should always remember to praise the child no matter how small the accomplishment may seem; in fact, even if the child has not yet achieved the desired result of the practice session, he should still be praised for effort. When a child takes a first step and then falls down, our excitement and encouragement create a desire to try and try again. These same responses should occur when a child is learning to play the piano. Many times physical rewards can help us to motivate children when they are not responding to praise. It is easier to offer a very young child a piece of candy in return for a good practice session than it is to argue and fuss for 20 minutes just trying to get him to the piano. As the child feels successful (because of the praise and encouragement) pride of accomplishment (self-esteem) is generally enough to maintain motivation.

Daily Practice   Practicing every day is of the utmost importance. Dr. Suzuki sometimes says to the children, "Only practice on the days that you eat." One young student took these words so seriously that after each meal, he would take his mother by the hand and go to the piano. It is also important to stress that only correct practicing is beneficial. If a child wants to experiment at the piano, there should be plenty of opportunity to do so. The message is: "Piano, I like you and I want to play with you." This is wonderful! It should not, however, be considered practicing.

Set Time for Practice   Establishing a regular time for practice every day is the best way to make sure that it is accomplished consistently. Children respond well to routine and if practicing can be a part of that routine, fewer problems and greater success will result. If this practice habit is established at the outset, it will help to carry the child through those inevitable plateaus that occur in the learning process.

Positive Reinforcement for Practice   Practicing should be a pleasurable and happy experience for the child. All human beings do their best when they are doing things they enjoy most; consequently if the children enjoy practicing they will learn better. Let the practicing be fun and this high spirit will carry through to high accomplishment. Children who practice well, play well, and the more they practice, the better they play. Dr. Suzuki says, "If you compare a person who practices five minutes a day with one who practices three hours, the difference is enormous even though they both practice daily. . . . If the five-minute-a-day person wants to accomplish what the three-hour-a-day person does, it will take him nine years. What one accomplishes in three months will take the other nine years."

One Thing at a Time   During the practice session the parent should ask for only one thing at a time. The child should have to think only about what has been requested. If the child accomplishes the task, but displays weaknesses in other aspects of the performance, he should still be highly praised. With daily correct practice, everything will soon fit together very easily. For example, perhaps a child can play a piece very well hands separately and is ready to play with both hands together. During the first attempts to put them together the beautiful technique suffers. This happens because the child's concentration is focused on putting hands together. When this coordination becomes easy, the teacher and parent can simply remind the child of the proper techniques. The piece will then be perfected easily. We do not correct the grammar of a baby first beginning to talk in sentences, but once he can use sentences well, we gently require proper usage.

The practice session should reinforce the main lesson point and if the child has a notebook with the specific number of repetitions marked, and the parent has a notebook with the goal clearly outlined, there should be no difficulty. Sometimes, however, even with the best intentions, unpleasant experiences occur during the practice sessions. After all, parents and children are only human! But try not to let the session end that way. It is best to finish practicing on a happy note. Glenn Doman, in *How to Teach Your Baby to Read* suggests that in order to maintain the interest of the child, *any* learning session should stop *before* the child tires of it. Then, the child will be eager to begin another learning session on another day or at a later time. In addition to stopping before the child tires, it is a good idea to end the session with something, perhaps a review piece, that the child can do very well.

The Role of Other Relatives at Home

Repetition is one of the most important elements in Suzuki education, and no matter how many times a child plays a piece, the parents must not show boredom. It may be difficult to be enthusiastic every time a child plays a piece or after the recording has been heard hundreds of times, but that is what a parent must do. It is better to motivate a child to repeat a piece or a segment of a piece by saying that he is doing so well that you love hearing it over and over again than it is just to say "Play it again." If negative attitudes, such as boredom, enter the home atmosphere, the student may balk at doing the many repetitions required for success. The story of Peeko (found in *Nurtured by Love,* p. 15) can reinforce this idea for parents. Siblings must also be encouraged to be supportive of each other's efforts.

Enthusiasm   Enthusiasm is probably the best antidote for negativeness. If parents can maintain enthusiasm for each step a child takes in the learning process, this spirit will be transmitted to the child and make him eager to try the next step.

Unpleasant Competitiveness   Unpleasant competitiveness should be discouraged. One should rejoice in one's own accomplishments, no matter how small they may seem and no matter how long they take. One child may have begun to talk at nine months and another may not have spoken until three years of age, however, as adults they can both communicate well and neither questions the other as to when the first words were uttered. Only the development of an ability is important, not when it was accomplished. We should try to teach our children to rejoice in the accomplishments of others as well and to realize that they have achieved their ability through diligence and work. They deserve the credit. The child must also know that he is making progress in the proper direction and that with work and patience will achieve the desired goal.

Anxiety   Parents should be careful not to cause anxiety before a lesson or performance by reminders of what to do. Instead, the child should be reminded of his accomplishments during the week. A parent must also avoid cramming too much into any practice session, particularly on the day before or the day of the lesson. This will simply overwhelm the child and perhaps cause anxiety at the lesson.

No Apologies   A parent should not apologize for the child either before or during the lesson. This is the same as the hostess who apologized to her guests all during dinner for all of her problems: the soup that was too salty, the overdone meat, the lumpy potatoes, *etc.* When leaving, one guest was overheard to say "I wish I had had the excruciating pleasure of finding out all those things for myself!" Please let the teacher have the pleasure of discovery also. The child may very well rise to the occasion and play well.

Musical Environment   Families should be encouraged to make music a common interest. Even very young children enjoy being taken to concerts if they do not have to stay too long. It is possible to go for only a portion of the program and leave before the child tires of it. Listening to recordings and classical radio programs creates a musical environment. One day in Corning, New York, several young Suzuki piano students heard Mozart's *Variations on "Ah! Vous Dirais-je Maman"* on the radio and were thrilled. In fact, one mother said that her child almost missed his school bus in order to hear the entire piece. What a thrill to observe a five-year-old responding so excitedly to music and what a motivation for learning the *Twinkle Variations*! Craig Timmerman, Suzuki music teacher, reminds us that "We should think of and instill MUSIC around the child all day long. PRACTICE IS A RESULT OF THE MUSICAL ENVIRONMENT."

Mini-Recitals   Mini-recitals at home during the week are a wonderful family experience. Some families set aside half an hour after dinner one night each week and the children play all the pieces they know for their parents. Asking children to play for guests is also a positive experience. Not only is it good practice for public performance, but it also builds the child's confidence and self-esteem. Having parents or siblings select pieces to be played at home concerts is a good way to accomplish review and make performing fun. This can be done as a game. Write the titles on small pieces of paper, fold them, and put them into a container. Then ask the child to play each piece that a family member draws.

Additional Parental Aids

In addition to clarifying the parents' roles, the teacher can help them in the following four ways:

Meetings

Regular meetings with the parents are very constructive. These meetings give the teacher an excellent opportunity to educate the parents in Dr. Suzuki's wonderful philosophy, to express appreciation of the parent's support, and to give gentle reminders of the attitudes or habits that need to be strengthened. It is much easier to make a quiet comment to the group on how much one appreciates punctuality at the lesson than to say directly to a tardy parent, "Why can't you be on time?" Dealing tactfully with the parents is an important part of a Suzuki teacher's job.

The meetings give the parents a chance to help each other; many parents have excellent ideas for those who are experiencing problems. Sometimes just airing problems helps morale because parents realize that others, too, have difficulties.

The meeting is a time for parents and teachers to discuss the child without the child's being present. It is important that the parents realize that discussing the child negatively *in front of him or her* is extremely damaging and should never be done!

Recommended Readings

In addition to *Nurtured by Love,* there are several excellent books which can help the parents learn how to work with their children better: *Between Parent and Child* by Haim Ginott, *How to Teach Your Baby to Read* by Glenn Doman, *Dibs in Search of Self* by Virginia M. Axeline and *Your Child's Self-Esteem* by Dorothy Corkille Briggs.

Maintenance of the Piano

Encourage the parents to keep the piano in tune and in good repair. The child will not be able to produce a good tone if the strings are out of tune and some of the notes will not sound. Imagine the frustration of trying to play tennis with a racquet that has broken strings or with balls that have little bounce left in them! One young child whose piano had many chipped and discolored keys could always begin pieces accurately at home. When he came to his lesson, he could never find the correct key because his orientation was based on a chipped key rather than on the black-key groupings.

The piano must be tuned to concert pitch ($A = 440\,Hz$) and maintained at this level with tunings at least twice, and preferably four times, a year. Not only will the instrument produce its best tone at this pitch, but the child will benefit from this consistent pitch level. Many Suzuki students develop absolute pitch or pitch recognition, a trait envied by many adult musicians, but this can only be accomplished with in-tune pianos. Pianos that are one quarter, one half, or occasionally one whole tone flat literally damage the child's musical ear or at least deprive the child of the chance to develop pitch recognition. Proper maintenance of an instrument, as with an automobile, also prolongs its life.

Purchase of a Tape Recorder

Encourage the family to purchase a quality cassette tape recorder. Thanks to modern technology, the cassette is one of the most valuable aids we have in our Suzuki teaching. Cassette recordings can be enjoyed on automobile trips, picnics, or in other situations where disc recordings cannot be used. Lessons can be recorded to aid the recall of the assignment or to help remotivate the child between lessons. Practice sessions may also be recorded. If parents, who are having problems during practice periods, record these sessions, the teacher is better able to help diagnose and solve the problems. Parents can also keep a record of progress via tape. When a young child masters a particular piece, it would be nice to record it for a replay five to ten years later. A tape of the child's playing can also make a lovely gift to a relative or friend.

The quality of the cassette recorder is most important. Just as a child can be harmed by playing an out-of-tune piano, an out-of-tune tape recorder can be equally detrimental. If the tape recorder will not maintain a constant speed, it will not play at a constant pitch. In *Nurtured by Love,* Dr. Suzuki says, "a baby absorbs perfectly any out-of-tune pitch of its mother's lullabies. It has a marvelous ear. That's why the child will later sing in the same way." We recommend that you purchase a high quality cassette recorder, use the same recorder for recording and play back, and always use fresh batteries or a fully charged battery pack when recording. Consider the purchase of a recorder that has a variable speed control on it so that the play back can be tuned to exact concert pitch (A = 440 *Hz*).

Conclusion

The greatest reward of parenthood is the joy of seeing your child become a fine, independent, and accomplished adult—one who has learned to set goals and master them. This ability carries over into all areas of life. Helping a child to acquire the skills and to develop the abilities necessary to succeed is the greatest gift a parent can give. To discover truth, virtue, and happiness is a worthy goal for any human being, but to help your child find the means to these goals is a gesture in loving in the most profound sense of the word.

Chapter 4

Motivating Students

Introduction

Motivating students is probably the greatest challenge and one of the most important responsibilities a teacher has.[4] A teacher must develop the child's desire to learn and practice. Once this desire is born, it must be kept alive until the student accepts the responsibility for his own learning. This is a challenging but rewarding task. Motivation is one of the keys to human accomplishment. Man does best when he is doing what he most enjoys doing and what he sincerely wants to do. Also he most enjoys doing those things which he does well. If a teacher can make a child eager to learn, any other problem is surmountable!

Since we believe that it is possible to learn and cultivate skills which motivate, we will discuss:

1. Motivational Attributes of the Teacher.
2. Actual Motivational Tools a Teacher Can Use.
3. Motivational Experiences a Teacher Can Provide for Children.

Motivational Attributes of the Teacher

Love and Respect

The first and most important attribute a teacher must have is genuine love and respect for the child as a human being. Children have emotions and sensitivities just as acute as those of adults. They are aware of people's feelings towards them and respond accordingly. If a teacher loves and respects a child, the child will in turn respect the teacher, and a good rapport is thus easy to establish. Dr. Haim G. Ginott, in *Between Teacher and Child* states, "To reach a child's mind, a teacher must first capture his heart."

As a way of demonstrating respect, a teacher should treat a child as she would any adult. With guests we never speak rudely or interrupt; neither should we interrupt a child who is either speaking or playing. If a child makes comments not related to the lesson, listen. Concentration will be better if the child has been allowed to clear his mind.

---

[4]We use the word teacher synonymously with parent because in Talent Education the parent's role is considered equal to that of the teacher. The parent must teach the child every day whereas the actual teacher works with the child only at lessons.

If a child is playing a piece for you, do not interrupt unless you are asked for help. Interruptions distract our own thinking and affect the children in the same way. Just because a child makes a mistake or hesitates does not necessarily mean that he is confused. Let the piece be finished and then work on problems. Imagine interrupting every time a speaker hesitates or says "Um!"

Through respect a teacher allows a child to develop and maintain self-esteem. Saving fact is important to adults, but is even more important to children. A teacher should take care not to let a child lose face (self-esteem). If this happens, very difficult and unpleasant situations can occur. One young, inexperienced teacher learned how upsetting a lesson can be when a child's pride is threatened. Two four-year-old boys shared a lesson time. One of the boys was aggressive and the other quiet and shy. The usual procedure had been to have the more extroverted child go first simply because he was always ready and eager. One day the aggressive child came to the lesson and firmly announced that he was not going to be first! The more reserved child stated that he wasn't either! The teacher and mothers tried every way possible to coax one of them into playing first. Since neither child wanted to give in, or even could, without losing face, the lesson ended with a multitude of tears shed by children, mothers, and teacher! The teacher could have avoided this confrontation completely by simply saying, "Okay, neither of you has to play first today. I will, and you can play second and third" (naming each child as she indicated his position). In this manner she would have shown respect for their decisions and hence eliminated any problem. A teacher should never try to command, order, or coax a child (just as we do not try to deal in this manner with adults), but simply ask, encourage, or guide in the desired direction.

Honesty

Along with the attribute of respect should come honesty. If we are not honest with people, children as well as adults, they will come to distrust us. A relationship without trust is not only nonproductive, it is ultimately destructive. An outstanding pediatrician was consistently able to earn the unquestioned trust and respect of all of his patients with his honesty. When children were due to have an innoculation, this doctor simply told them that it would hurt. He then instructed them to yell "Ouch" as loudly as they could when they felt the hurt. He did not lie to the children by telling them that they would not feel anything, nor did he try to distract them by carrying on an irrelevant conversation or by having them close their eyes. The children always knew what to expect when they came to his office. Because they trusted and respected him, they were never frightened or humiliated by crying out when the shot that wasn't supposed to hurt, really did!

Patience

One often hears the comment that one must have a great deal of patience in dealing with children. Webster defines the word patience as: "Bearing or enduring pains, trials or the like, without complaint or with equanimity.'' Patience may often be a quality of good teachers, but the teacher who loves and respects students and who reacts with understanding finds that dealing with children is a joy and not a trial!

Empathy

The teacher must be empathetic, able to sense and respond to the needs and moods of the student. On occasion a child comes to a lesson following an unhappy experience some time during that day or week. That child could, consequently, be unresponsive or even negative and perhaps be brought to tears easily. If the teacher can sense the mood and offer gentleness and understanding, the lesson is more apt to be productive. It is also helpful if the teacher knows of any unusual family circumstances that may affect the child. One student came to a lesson and was unable to concentrate until she finally blurted out that her pet hamster had died that morning. The teacher therefore spent part of the lesson working on a sad song (*e.g., Chant Arabe*) to lament the death of the hamster. Because the teacher was able to extend sympathy and understanding, the lesson was successful.

Often an incident which seems trivial to an adult is serious to a child. A teacher must try to appreciate what the child is feeling. Samuel Johnson in *Boswell's Life of Dr. Johnson* expresses this attitude beautifully: ''Nothing is little to him that feels it with great sensibility.''

Enthusiasm

The final and very necessary attitude a teacher must have in motivating children is enthusiasm. How can we excite a child if we ourselves are unexcited? If our greeting is spirited, the child will be happy to see us and to play for us. We must react with enthusiasm towards the child no matter how we feel. Our enthusiasm not only creates the mood for the lesson but creates in the child a desire to play and to practice. In reference to a performing artist, one often hears the comment that ''he was really *up* for this concert.'' Our spirit and enthusiasm are the greatest attributes we can cultivate in order to motivate our students.

We must also be enthusiastic about the music. If we show delight for each and every piece in the repertoire, our attitude will be contagious. Some students tend to balk at reviewing early selections, especially after they have advanced into later volumes, but if we can convey our enthusiasm for these pieces, the child well be delighted to please us. In addition to being enthusiastic about the music, we can also relate our love for the piano to children by saying, ''Piano, I like you and when I play with you, you will sing to me!'' Children love playing with the piano—experimenting and creating—just as much as they enjoy playing with a favorite toy. We should encourage this play while still being careful to make the distinction between experimenting and practicing.

Actual Motivational Tools a Teacher Can Use

Reward

In addition to attributes a teacher can develop, there are many useful motivational tools. Reward is one of the simplest and best motivational tools available and praise is the best reward we can give. Everyone responds positively to praise, and if we conscientiously offer praise, the child's desire to please us will increase if for no other reason than that he knows it is possible. Praise instills confidence; confidence builds a desire to try; the desire to try develops the ability to learn; the ability to learn leads to accomplishment; and accomplishment earns praise. This is a self-perpetuating cycle which can be initiated effectively by a teacher.

Praise We should always tell a child what we liked about a performance, and we can always find something, no matter how small. A teacher, however, should be honest with praise. Never praise a child for something not done well. Children have high standards for themselves and lying to them will only destroy your own credibility. If the child has not been able to accomplish the assignment perfectly, we should still lavishly praise the effort made and try to make the next task within easy reach of the child. The teacher must always find a point to praise because our praise will encourage further work, and no comment at all could be discouraging. Also, be sure to give special praise for the accomplishment of last week's assignment or for the improvement of a weakness.

No Criticism While consciously remembering to praise a child one must also be careful not to criticise. Children need help and guidance, not criticism. One child after a piano lesson told her mother that the teacher spent most of the time finding fault with her piece. This very perceptive child asked her mother, "How did all of her fault-finding help me to play better?" We can all remember teachers who never said a positive word, and we soon realized that anything we tried to do was not good enough, so we simply gave up and stopped trying. Praise encourages and negativism discourages. When a child first tries to walk and falls down after a few steps, we are not negative, we show our delight in the effort, encourage new attempts, and offer support. When a child cannot do something well at the piano, we should simply show how to do it better, with praise for trying. One of the greatest obstacles to learning is a child's fear of humiliation either by criticism or failure.

Material Rewards In addition to praise, we can sometimes use material rewards. These are not as good as praise and encouragement and should be reserved for those times when a little extra boost is needed. Children love stickers and stars, and these symbols give the child not only the pleasure of the reward, but also the opportunity to show friends and family at home proof of success. For very special occasions like the completion of a book, something like a lollipop can add to the celebration atmosphere.

Humor

Another motivational tool a teacher can use is humor. Children respond positively to laughter and fun, and if a teacher creates a happy atmosphere, the student will enjoy the lessons and learn better. This is evidenced in the very first lessons as we watch the smiles appear when we use silly words like Mississippi Hot Dog to describe the rhythms in the *Twinkle Variations*. When using humor, a teacher must be careful not to use sarcasm. Children do not yet understand the subtleties of negative humor and may find it frightening.

Specific Techniques

Another way to motivate the child is to make all requests and assignments as specific as possible. A student who knows exactly what is expected is better able to accomplish the assignment. It is better to ask that something be played ten times a day than simply to say that it should be practiced many times every day. Many is vague; ten is specific. In this manner we can establish repetition and help the parent make reasonable demands on the child during any one practice session. The teacher can write the number of repetitions in the child's notebook and thus help to organize his practicing.

Notebooks   We suggest that each child bring his own notebook to lessons so that the teacher can write down each week's assignment. In this notebook we not only write what to practice but also how many times each piece or segment should be played daily. This specific written assignment avoids wasted effort at the piano, and also helps the student use time efficiently. It is useless to have a child sit at the piano for a half hour if he is able to concentrate for only ten minutes or if there is no specific goal towards which to work. If the child knows exactly what is expected, he will feel more secure and be more strongly motivated.

Charts   Making practice charts for young children is an aid to both the child and the parent. Charts appeal to children who can thereby readily determine where they are in their practice and how much more they have to do. If the teacher asks a student to play an assignment ten times a day, for example, the child may prefer to do five repetitions at one session and complete the other five later. Marking each repetition on a chart not only gives a sense of accomplishment but also organizes work in the proper direction. At the next lesson the teacher can place a star on the chart in recognition of the child's work. Children love these charts so much that they will often pressure their parents into practicing just so they can fill them up! Charts are especially effective with students whose parents are not always conscientious about practice time.

Demonstration   To be specific, the teacher should also use as much demonstration and as little verbalization as possible. Children lose interest with too much talk, and grasp concepts better when they are shown rather than told how. Imagine how difficult it would be to teach a child how to tie shoes with only an explanation and no step-by-step demonstration!

Who helped me							
Date	Thurs.	Fri.	Sat.	Sun.	Mon.	Tues.	Wed.
Sightreading							
Technique							
Suzuki piece							
Preview							
Review #1							
Review #2							
Listening to Record							
Remarks (Positive Comments from the Teacher)							

Practice Record Chart

How Music Grows—Peach Tree Analogy

Goals   We also like to tell a child exactly how much of a piece has been accomplished and where he is in relation to a polished work. This is a specific goal. We describe the stages of learning using the following comparison with a peach tree:

Stage 1. Learning notes and memorizing = the peach blossom.
Stage 2. Polishing (details) = the peach forming and growing.
Stage 3. Seasoning (living with the music for a while) = the hard green peach gradually turning to sweet sugary pulp.
Stage 4. Perfection = a perfect, ready-to-eat, peach.

Successes   The fourth motivational tool we can use is success—one of the most natural motivations for all people. As Dr. Suzuki teaches, "Ability breeds ability." Ability is success and success motivates. If a teacher makes sure that a child is always successful, that child will be inspired to continue working. In order to ensure this success, a teacher must be certain that a child can do the assignment very well before leaving the lesson. If the student cannot, frustration will tarnish the lessons and practice sessions, and the child will begin to balk. One must be especially sure to set attainable goals for the child while still giving enough work to be stimulating. Children often misbehave or refuse to try if they think that they cannot do what was asked of them. If the goal or task is too difficult or too long for the child, the teacher must reduce it to a smaller step. For example, if the student is working on one phrase and cannot grasp it, the teacher should reduce it to one measure. Being successful means having the ability to attain one's desired goal, and since we can nurture ability, we can ensure success.

In order to ensure success, we must make an accurate assessment of each child's ability. Being able to diagnose problems and pace teaching is one of the most difficult aspects of our job. Without thinking, many teachers tell a child that a piece is easy to play. This kind of statement can be very dangerous because if the child does not find it easy, he will feel inadequate or even stupid. It is better to tell a child that something is hard and then if the task is accomplished easily, the child will feel like a stronger and better person. On the other hand, if we tell a child that something is hard and it is not, our honesty may be questioned.

Motivational Experiences a Teacher Can Provide for Children

Games

In addition to the tools we have suggested, a teacher can provide many experiences that motivate children. These experiences can take the form of games which are created to aid review, memory, and concentration. The games can also be used in testing a child's understanding, or in group and performance situations. Some educators resist games or gimmicks. However, we feel that anything that makes learning easier and more fun is definitely an aid to teaching. One must be careful not to let the fun become uncontrolled and interfere with the lesson. Many children are distracted by too much play, but if a teacher uses this type of experience judiciously and with a specific purpose in mind, many problems can be solved easily. A teacher's imagination can invent any number of games and experiences that motivate learning.

Fish Game   Review is one of the most important elements of Suzuki education, and there are many ways to have fun while reviewing. One can create many variations of a game which we call Fish. The teacher or parent can write the title of the review pieces on cards or slips of paper (sketch a picture for children who do not yet read). Have the child draw one card from a box and play the piece drawn. Some teachers even use magnetised cards and a fishing pole to make this game more realistic. If one does not have the time or talent to do this sort of thing, simply assigning a number to each piece and having friends, siblings, or parents choose numbers accomplishes the same purpose.

A Story   Learning all of Volume 1 represents a milestone for Suzuki piano students and is cause for celebration. In our teaching, when the student completes this volume, we have a "party lesson" during which the student performs the entire volume. To make the occasion more festive we have written the following story which incorporates the title of every piece in Volume 1. The teacher reads the story aloud and as each title occurs, the narrator stops and the student performs that piece. When the story is finished, we conclude the lesson and celebrate by giving the student a cupcake with a lighted candle in it.

"Once upon a time there was a little boy named *Allegro* who woke up one morning to the sound of his *Cuckoo* clock. When he went downstairs, his mother said, 'I have a *Christmas Day Secret.*' The secret was that *Mary Had a Little Lamb.* While whistling a tune called *Allegretto 2,* the little boy quickly ran to see the lamb. He and Mary decided to show the lamb to their *Little Playmates.* On their way, they came to the river and exclaimed: '*London Bridge is Falling Down!* We must *Go Tell Aunt Rhody.*' Because the bridge was dangerous, they had to climb into their boat and *Lightly Row* across the river.

After crossing the river, they came to a field and stopped to listen to a piper playing his *Musette;* however, they were able to stop only briefly because a *Honey Bee* was beginning to annoy their lamb. As they approached the school where their aunt was teaching, they heard the *French Children's Song* filling the air with music. They entered the building just as the music lesson was ending with *Clair de Lune.* They told their aunt the tale of the broken bridge. Their aunt thanked them for the news and explained that since the bridge was built so *Long, Long Ago,* she was not surprised. She suggested that they report the problem to Mr. *Chant Arabe,* after which she bid them *Adieu.*

They did as they were told and then hurried home to their mother. After telling their story and having a good dinner, their mother rocked the children to sleep humming *Allegretto 1* and tucked them into their beds. As the excitement of the day danced in the children's dreams, the skies also seemed to dance with a myriad of *Twinkle, Twinkle Little Star Variations.*"

Looking forward to this "party lesson" encourages consistent review. Several lessons preceding the celebration are therefore devoted to a thorough review of every piece so that the child becomes confident and comfortable, and the party is a great success.

Role Reversal Reversing roles is another game which works well for children who seem to be having difficulty with a piece. Most

children dislike being tested. When they know that they can do something, they really do not care if the teacher knows. Often they just do not want to concentrate or show us what they can do. Sometimes a parent tells the teacher that a child is having trouble with a particular piece at home, but when the child plays it for the teacher, it is perfect. This is probably because the child did not want to play it correctly for his parents. This situation can also easily happen at a lesson, and we suggest that the teacher ask the student to trade roles. The student must then be teacher. The teacher then pretends to have difficulty and the child must help. If the child can help the teacher do the assigned task properly, he probably understands it. The teacher can then ask the child to demonstrate how to play the entire piece correctly. This is a good method of testing the child's understanding without an obvious test! The parent can use this technique at home as well. He or she can either pretend to have forgotten the teacher's instructions and ask the child for help or the child can be asked to teach another family member to do the assignment.

Scramble Game   If a child is having memory problems or difficulty learning the sequence of the parts of a piece, we suggest using a game we call Scramble. We divide a piece into phrases (or sections for longer pieces) and number each section. We then practice one section at a time referring to it by its designated number. When the student knows it well and can distinguish as few as two phrases, we write the numbers 1 and 2 on separate slips of paper. Fold the papers and ask the student to select and then play the one drawn. We follow this procedure for the whole piece, and if the child can play it scrambled, there will certainly be no problem in playing it correctly in order. This game works well for pieces at all levels. For example, the Bach *Prelude in C Major* in Volume 5 is difficult to memorize, but teaching it using Scramble has eliminated memory problems for the children. Scramble is also an excellent technique for developing concentration because a child has to think very carefully about which phrase (2, 6, or whichever) is the one which was drawn. In addition to these benefits, it enables the student to begin the piece at many points. This is quite helpful when studying or teaching the longer, more advanced repertoire.

Freeze   For children who have difficulty concentrating or just sitting still long enough to play a piece, we like to use a game we call Freeze. To use this technique, have the child position his hands at the keyboard and get ready to begin the piece. The teacher then says "Freeze" and the child must hold that position until the freeze is broken. The count of five breaks the freeze. A teacher can freeze a child at any point in the piece either to check the correct hand position or to prepare the child for a difficult technique. This game is actually an excellent way to make an enjoyable activity of the STOP-PREPARE technique we use in teaching all of the repertoire.

Clap Game   Many children who have perfected a piece have memory blocks during a performance. Sometimes something as simple as a wrong fingering can trigger a memory slip. We like to prepare children for this sort of situation by giving them concrete suggestions which can help solve the problem in a concert. A pianist does not have the benefit of an accompanist who can help bring back the memory, and we have all seen situations where a child has a problem which causes so much distress that a chain reaction of problems is started. The student makes a mistake and then thinks and worries about it instead of concentrating on what he is playing; so another mistake is made and so on.

In order to prevent this chain reaction, we play what we call the Clap Game. As the child is playing a piece, the teacher claps at any point (practice only). The child must then immediately go back or ahead to a phrase or section that is nearest to where the teacher clapped or where the problem occurred. If the child has studied with the scramble technique, going back is easy. The child must do this without stopping for more than a few seconds. If this is practiced at home and at the lesson, the child, when he gets into difficulty during a performance, will act positively and decisively rather than react to the mistake. In order to make a child feel comfortable about doing this in a concert, we say: If all of the children in your class were asked to write a story, and your story was picked as the best one—in fact, the best one that any of the teachers had ever seen—but you spelled three words incorrectly, those three misspelled words would not spoil the story! The same is true in piano. If you are playing in a concert and you make a few mistakes but the music was still beautiful, you would not have spoiled the piece. People are aware only of the beauty of the music and do not remember mistakes.

Miracles

In addition to games, we have found that our responses to new discoveries or experiences motivate. In Talent Education we know that all children can learn a great deal easily and without any help (especially sounding out new pieces). They can do this because of their ear training; however, when a child can do something easily and independently, we call it a Miracle! Miracles motivate, so we must rejoice abundantly. One example of what we call a miracle is a child being able to harmonize a tune solely by ear. A student who learns *Go Tell Aunt Rhody* can usually play *Twinkle* with an Alberti accompaniment. Ask the child to try this, and when he is successful, call it a miracle! It is a builder of self-esteem. Children love to discover things for themselves and when they do, they feel successful. If we recognize their success with much celebration, they will be highly motivated.

Group Experiences

Finally, a teacher can use group experiences to motivate. A teacher should try to have regular classes or group sessions where children can play for each other and learn concert behavior in an informal situation. Recitals or concerts also serve as special motivation by providing a specific goal and a special occasion. We suggest having a public performance at least once a year to give students a chance to invite friends and relatives to hear them play. We also encourage them to attend workshops and institutes because they receive high stimulation and great motivation from these experiences.

These group experiences motivate in many ways. First, they provide a specific reason for practice and for perfection of a piece. Some children will even practice especially well throughout the year in the hopes of reaching and polishing a particular piece in time to play at a recital or workshop. When the *student* sets such a long-range goal, motivation is never a problem! Second, children also receive inspiration from this kind of experience because they hear other, more advanced students; but they also gain confidence because they hear students who are less advanced. Third and perhaps most important of all, the classes, recitals, and institutes are pleasant social experiences. It is a thrilling sight to watch a group of children relating happily with one another with good music as their common interest.

Summary

Motivation provided the impetus to eliminate smallpox and to put men on the moon. Our most important responsibility as teachers is to provide the impetus for learning. If a teacher loves and respects children, praise, enthusiasm, and empathy will come as natural means to motivate. If a teacher conscientiously implements these natural elements with humor, specific instructions, successes, rewards, games, miracles, and group experiences, the environment for learning will be sound and children will achieve great ability with eagerness and ease.

Chapter 5

Structuring an Effective Lesson

Introduction

Structure is present in every part of human life. The body is the physical structure in which we live and the family, city, state, and nation are the social structures through which we relate. Without these structures life would be chaos and confusion. It is only through structure and organization that one can gain the freedom to create and to accomplish.

Structure in a lesson means having a form or plan. If we, as teachers, do not have a specific plan for each child and a meaningful direction towards which that child can aim, our end results will not be good, nor even satisfactory. In Suzuki education, as in other music methods, it is very easy to fall into the trap of simply following the printed order which is already so well-organized for us. This material supplies our basic structure, but in order to teach effectively, we must be as well-organized in our approach and our procedures as are the materials we use. We must decide on our goals for each student, not only so that we can use our teaching time most effectively, but also so that we can better direct the student's own efforts towards maximum achievement.

All skills are learned on a step-by-step basis. These skills include everything from teaching a baby to use a spoon to an advanced course in calculus. Since playing the piano is a complex skill, it is essential to have a well-organized lesson structure. The following ideas for structuring an effective lesson will include:

1. Definition of an Effective Lesson.
2. Elements of a Lesson.
3. Actual Presentation of the Lesson.
4. Clarification of the Lesson.

Definition of an Effective Lesson

An effective lesson should raise the child's self-esteem.

Raise the Child's Self-Esteem

A child who feels good about himself will be more receptive to learning. Praising the child for what can already be done well is probably the easiest way to establish self-confidence. Since the child will do some things well, but not everything, be sure to recognize any accomplishment however small it may seem.

Motivate the Student

An effective lesson should make the child eager to try a new challenge (most probably the coming week's assignment). At this point the child is moving from the known to the unknown. If the new step is mastered and understood at the lesson, the child will be able to work at home without frustration. The mastery and the resulting confidence gained at the lesson will serve as motivation for the week.

Create a Desire to Reach the Next Goal.

An effective lesson should create a desire to reach the next goal. One traditional teacher actually spent weeks building excitement in the students about their first Bach book before giving it to them. About a month before the teacher planned to introduce Bach, the children would be told each week that they were almost advanced enough for the Bach book. By the time they got the book, they were so excited that no additional motivation was needed, and the frustration that normally comes from the first attempts to play counterpoint were replaced by the thrill of a new challenge. Another Suzuki teacher stimulated this desire to advance to a new step by telling a child, who had mastered a piece hands separately, that he had "earned the privilege to play the piece hands together!" This was good psychology because if a child thinks of a new and difficult technique as a privilege, it will not be considered a chore!

Elements of a Lesson

A good lesson must *cover all of the elements of a lesson* and the best way to do this is to have a definite and recognizable plan. Children thrive on structure because it provides security. If a child knows what will be expected at the lesson, he will feel secure and behave appropriately. Disorganization on the part of a teacher can be very disconcerting to a child. One teacher asked a child to go home and practice A, B, and C, and when the child came to the lesson the following week, the teacher asked him to play X, Y, and Z! This kind of situation can be very upsetting to children. When a child is asked for something unexpected he becomes insecure. We all remember sitting in a classroom in school eagerly waving our hands in the air when we knew the answer to a question; and we also remember shrinking in our seats trying to hide when we did not. A good lesson should never cause a child to shrink back. Structure, however, does not mean rigidity. Sometimes a teacher may have to spend a considerable amount of lesson time working on a difficult passage. If this occurs, the teacher should not be concerned about having to skip an item or two until the next week. It is much better to send a child home secure with less material than it is to cover every item, sacrificing thoroughness for the sake of structure.

Long-Term Plan for the Student

A lesson should *be a clear and essential part of the long-term plan for that child.* If you do not know where you are going, you may arrive back where you started. A teacher must know the levels of the child's abilities in relation to the goal. Imagine how useless a map would be if you did not know where you were! You could not find the road that would lead you to your desired destination. If we do not have a planned route and destination for a child, we cannot guide his progress in the correct direction.

Elements of a Lesson

Each lesson should consist of the following four segments:

1. Note-Reading.
2. Technique.
3. Suzuki Material.
4. Review.

Each of these elements will be discussed separately so that a clearer idea of what is done can be illustrated. An example which indicates the approximate amounts of time to be spent on each element is included on page 91. Please remember that these timings will vary from lesson to lesson.

Note-Reading

Since the inability to read music is one of the main but unnecessary criticisms of Talent Education students, note-reading should be included in every lesson as soon as the child is ready to learn this skill. There are two reasons for using the first few minutes of lesson time to teach reading. First, it is a separate skill and is referred to as such. It requires a different brain function than the other segments of the lesson, thus it is easier for the child to separate functions according to the types of concentration required. Second, the habit of beginning the lesson with reading should be established because it is easy to exhaust the lesson time before ever getting to it. The number of minutes spent on note-reading is less critical than the fact that it occurs at every lesson. Reserving these few minutes in the beginning of the lesson is much the same as putting money in savings as soon as the paycheck arrives rather than saving what is left at the end of the pay period. The slow steady saver will eventually gain more, as will the student who slowly but consistently spends time reading. The procedures and materials used to teach reading will be discussed in Chapter 6.

Technique

The second segment of the lesson is devoted to technique. This also takes only a few minutes to accomplish and should be done regularly at the beginning of the lesson. Teaching technique at this time helps the child to warm up his hands and fingers, and to adjust to a different instrument. Since the touch and action on every piano are unique, having a chance to play a few warm-up exercises or technical studies helps the student make the adjustment from the piano at home to the one used for the lesson. The procedure for introducing and teaching technique will be discussed in detail in Chapter 7.

Suzuki Material

The Suzuki material should by all means be the major part of the lesson. The teacher should:

a. Hear Last Week's Assignment.
b. Work on the Current Assignment.
c. Introduce the Preview Material.

Hear Last Week's Assignment Last week's assignment should be perfectly mastered when the student plays it at the lesson. If this assignment was within easy reach, and the child has practiced regularly, there is usually no problem. Suzuki often repeats, "One step at a time," and if teachers conscientiously follow his advice, this one step is always small enough for the child to accomplish in one week. Repetition of the new work should be the *only* task for the child at home. After the student has demonstrated mastery of the step which he has been practicing all week, give abundant praise. The combination of lesson mastery and the teacher's recognition of it will prepare the child both technically and psychologically for the next step.

Work on the Current Assignment This is the most important part of the lesson because the child is moving from the known to the unknown. This material should be presented so well and so clearly that the child has a 95 percent chance of succeeding when he practices it at home. If the child cannot do what you are asking at the lesson, the step may be too big. It may contain more steps than you realize and the number of steps must then be reduced. Some children can grasp as much as a phrase at a time while others may be able to handle only one measure or less.

If the steps have been reduced to as few as possible and the child still cannot perform the expected task, he may be trying to think of too many things at once. If this is the case, assure the child that you care only about what he is trying to accomplish and nothing else. For example, if the student is concentrating on the coordination of hands together and the hand position suffers, ignore the hand position and comment only on the coordination. Never expect a child to concentrate on more than one thing at a time.

If the child is still not able to do what is asked after the steps are made smaller and concentration is directed in only one area, the teacher may be presenting the material in a way not compatible with the child's present level of understanding. This is simply a communication problem, and the teacher must then explain or demonstrate in a different way. Many times we feel that we have explained a detail clearly, but that clarity is based on our own understanding within our own frame of reference. One five-year-old was having a lesson on the very beginning of *Cuckoo,* and the teacher could not get the child to play the opening measure twice. After many different approaches to the problem, the example was finally played perfectly when the teacher, out of sheer desperation, said "Play it two times!" Obviously the child simply did not know the meaning of twice.

When the child can do what you have asked, show your pleasure through lavish praise. The child must feel the joy of success so that he will go home and practice with ease and confidence, motivated by the teacher's response. One teacher refused to respond positively to the successes of her students because she felt that praise would make the child think he was good and therefore did not have to work. Such a negative attitude crushes the joy we all like to feel when we have accomplished something, no matter what it is! In addition to praise, we must also repeat the new step many times at the lesson in order to be sure that the child did not do it correctly by accident! At home the child should need only repetition, not learning, on that particular step.

When the child is able to play the piece hands together without technical problems, the piece can be refined musically. This means dynamics, phrasing, mood, tempo, balance, and musical form. Refining the music can either be done at the same lesson or reserved for the next lesson if there were many technical problems. In other words, the material for the new week can be technical, musical, or both. A child who is not secure with technique or memory, will not be able to concentrate on musical refinements.

Musical expression and sensitivity can be grasped by children very early in their experience. For example, they can easily create the echo effect in *Twinkle,* and many can feel the graduated dynamics in *Lightly Row.* Children love to add expression, and encouraging this ability is one of the advantages of Suzuki education. Because they are not dependent on the printed page, the students are free to think about musical expression.

Introduce the Preview Material   Technically difficult segments of a forthcoming piece should be carefully selected by the teacher and previewed with the student. (Suggestions on what to preview will be offered in the discussions of the repertoire, Chapters 9 through 14.) The advantages of previewing are many. First, if the children have learned and mastered the difficulties in a forthcoming piece, the remainder is easier to learn when they reach that piece. Second, because they have invested enough time with these technical problems, they also have more confidence when they begin the study of the new piece. This preview also whets the appetite for the piece— something like the coming attractions at the movies. Third, preview allows thorough mastery of a very small part. This creates good habits. One student who learned too much without adequate preparation suffered a great deal of frustration because it was so very difficult to unlearn the incorrect habits and replace them with correct ones. We have all been in situations where a technically difficult portion of a piece caused us to have problems, not only with the technique, but also with the nervous tension which the fear of these sections caused. With proper preview, technical difficulties and the psychological problems caused by them can be essentially eliminated.

Review

The last part of the lesson should be devoted to review pieces. Reviewing previously learned pieces is one of the most important and representative aspects of Suzuki education. In traditional methods, children tend to learn a piece, play it on a few occasions and then forget it. In Talent Education, the student constantly reviews, refreshes, and improves the repertoire. Review in the piano program, however, presents a problem which is different from the violin program. Violinists are able to participate in group sessions, and therefore have the benefit of reviewing a great deal of music. In piano group sessions, each child must play alone. Thus, the violin student may review ten pieces in one hour but the pianist will typically do only one. The violinist also has the help of the group and the accompanist when memory problems occur. The pianist must be totally self-dependent for all memory and confidence. Because review at the piano is more time-consuming and more difficult to continue, it is helpful to include it as a regular part of the lesson.

Ideally all the pieces a child has learned should be kept at concert readiness. Reviewing from *Twinkle* through the end of Volume 1 is entirely practical and possible. It takes only 20 minutes to play all of the first volume, which, if the child has been working consistently, will not be impossible. Most conscientious students review every piece every day. When the students progress to later volumes, however, there is far too much material to review daily.

Because reviewing is a problem for the advanced student, the teacher should assign a specific review piece each week. Since some of the sonatas last at least ten minutes without any work on difficulties, one movement would probably be enough for a review assignment. If the pieces to be reviewed are short, it is possible to assign as many as three. If a piece needs more work to bring it up to the proper musical level, assign only a portion of it or assign it for two consecutive weeks. A teacher must carefully rotate the selection of review pieces, because it is very easy to choose only one's own favorites.

Never reprimand a child for forgetting a piece. Remember—review should be fun for the child, and even a concert artist would find it difficult to keep several volumes of music at a concert level of mastery at all times!

A repertoire list made up of a variety of selections from all of the volumes is another aid for promoting review of a reasonable number of pieces. If the student is reading music well at this point, it is not necessary to include pieces from Volume 1. Have the student play through each of the pieces on the list at least twice a week just to review the notes. If a performance opportunity arises, it will be quite easy to polish these pieces in just a few days. On the other hand, most children will retain the musical expression while they are reviewing the notes. Asking families to have private home concerts can make review of the repertoire list even more pleasurable for the child.

There are many games that can make review fun. These games are described in Chapter 4—*Motivating Students*. If, however, review is impossible, conscientious listening to the records is very beneficial. Many children forget a great deal of repertoire when they are away on summer vacation, but if they can take their tape recorders with them, they will forget far less. Ask students to listen not only to their current volume but to the past ones as well. This review listening will help the recall of pieces that have not been played for a long time.

With the review piece, we conclude the lesson. Psychologically this is a positive experience for the child because it means that he always ends the lesson with success, and therefore goes home feeling good about himself and the lesson. Young students love to end the lesson with a *Twinkle* duet, the teacher playing an elaborate accompaniment to the child's performance. Students love this so much that they invariably move over on the bench to make room for the teacher without even being reminded. Anything that sends a child home from the lesson in a highly motivated state is a sign of successful teaching. The main purpose of teaching is to generate enthusiasm and to facilitate learning. Review is generally the best motivation because the child is comfortable with an old, accomplished piece. Saving the best for last is the reason dessert is eaten at the end of the meal—the good taste can last longest! An example of the pacing of a half hour lesson, including all of the elements is as follows:

Note Reading   — 5 minutes
Technique   — 3–5 minutes
Suzuki Material   — 15–19 minutes
Review   — 3–5 minutes

Clarification of the Lesson

To make sure that each and every lesson is as effective as possible, we suggest using a notebook system. We use three different notebooks: one for the teacher, one for the student, and one for the parent. Writing things down promotes organization, clarifies specific goals and procedures, develops consistency, and enhances understanding by all.

Teacher's Notebook

The teacher's notebook serves as a private reference and as a log recording the student's progress. Each student should be evaluated, noting strengths as well as weaknesses that need attention and concentration. If a teacher has goals for the student, it takes only a few seconds after each lesson to jot down comments relating to these goals. These notes are *only* for the teacher and may include such things as problems of technique, memory, performance, or personality (*e.g.,* lack of confidence). Writing these things on paper helps clarify both the problems and the successes, and ensures proper recognition of each. Evaluating students will make it easier to diagnose their difficulties. A good teacher, like a good doctor, must be a good diagnostician. A problem must be isolated before it can be solved.

Student's Notebook

The student's notebook is his or her own property. It should be brought to the lesson each week so that the teacher can write down the assignments. In addition to writing the assignment, the teacher can assign a specific number of repetitions for each day. Dr. Suzuki says, "5,000 times if we need it, but maybe you will only need 3,000 times." The teacher can quote and expand on Dr. Suzuki's statement to establish the advantages to be gained by many repetitions. A specific assignment helps the child to organize daily practice and direct it toward a specific goal. It also helps the student to see exactly what is expected. It helps parents during the practice sessions because the instructions have come directly from the teacher. Children will generally do what the teacher asks more willingly than they will do what their parent asks. At the lesson this notebook will prevent the teacher from asking the child to play something that has not been practiced. It also ensures that all elements will be included in each lesson.

Parent's Notebook

An important adjunct to the parent's presence at the lesson is his or her notebook. It should be brought to every lesson for the purpose of noting the teacher's comments and suggestions so that the parent will be better equipped to help the child at home. The parent must understand that the teacher's lesson with the child is the model for the practice at home, and must feel free to ask questions if the assignment is unclear. With the written comments to aid recall, the parent will be better able to help the child complete the assignment as accurately as possible each day. The parent can also easily encourage the child to look forward to the teacher's pleasure at the new mastery. Writing things down always eliminates confusion between what a teacher actually said and what the child may have erroneously remembered. In other words, the parent will have written proof of the teacher's suggestions which often have more authority to the child than the parent's word! In addition to taking notes, the parent must be sure to understand the techniques the child is expected to accomplish. If there is confusion, the teacher should spend a few minutes of the lesson time at the piano with the parent.

Conclusion

It is possible to sew a dress, bake a cake, or build a house without a plan, but success is far more likely if a plan is followed. It is also possible to teach a child how to play the piano without an organized structure, but again a structure makes success far more likely. We therefore believe that a teacher will achieve excellent results if the lesson plan is followed; if all elements in the lesson are included; and if the lesson is clear to the child, the teacher, and the parent. With this approach, every lesson will be a joy for all concerned.

Chapter 6

Technique

Introduction

Every activity, from hammering a nail to playing the piano, requires a special technique. These techniques may be discovered by the individual for himself, but this is a slow and usually very inefficient process. Most novices learn necessary techniques from imitation at first and later by association. This is by far the most efficient way of learning.

The greater the technique a person possesses in a complex skill, the greater are the possibilities for creativity. In order to play the piano, a creative art which requires physical skills, technique must be mastered to the point where the muscles react automatically to a stimulus from the brain. It is only then that the performer is free to think about the musical interpretation.

What Is Technique?

Technique to the pianist involves three things. The elements of piano sounds (legato, *portato,* staccato, *etc.*) must be isolated; how these sounds combine in different kinds of music must be studied; and the pianist must analyze what movements of the arm, the hand, and the fingers must be made to produce the desired sounds. In addition, certain patterns of pitches emerge in our common heritage of music—Baroque, Classical, Romantic, Impressionist, and Contemporary. These patterns, scales and arpeggios, may be practiced independently so that when they occur within a piece of music, they may be more quickly and easily assimilated.

"But," the novice Suzuki teacher cries, "I thought teaching Suzuki was supposed to eliminate all of that tedious practicing of scales and arpeggios that stifled love of music in children!" The answer is yes, Suzuki has eliminated the tedium, and no, he has not eliminated the practicing of technique. Dr. Suzuki has cleverly devised a way of introducing technique to the children, technique that they willingly practice over and over again, enjoying every bit of the process.

Technique in Suzuki, Volume One

Piano technique is introduced in *Twinkle, Twinkle, Little Star*—a piece that has been loved by generations of people in many different countries. Dr. Suzuki chose this theme because it was familiar to most parents. This, he reasoned, would create a pleasant bond between parent and child in their introduction to music. He developed a set of variations on this theme which contain most of the elements of technique required for Baroque and Classical repertoire. The *Twinkle Variations* are pure technique disguised as a piece. While children are learning these variations, they are, without realizing it, developing and practicing their first technical assignments at the piano.

Twinkle Variations

(See Chapter 9—Studying Volume 1 for a discussion on how to present these to the students.)

Variation A   (Mississippi Hot Dog). This employs two different types of staccato: 1) forearm staccato (Hot Dog) and 2) small wrist staccato (Mississippi). For a more detailed discussion of this technique, see Chapter 8—*The First Lessons.*

Variation B   (Bounce Roll Bounce). In our opinion this is the most difficult variation to teach and the most crucial one. (See Chapter 9—Studying Volume 1). The Bounce, a forearm staccato motion, is combined with a longer held note, the Roll, in which the child is asked to roll the wrist forward. This is followed by another Bounce note. It is the rolling motion that is difficult both to describe and to teach. We recommend that all teachers unfamiliar with this technique attend a workshop because a demonstration eliminates any confusion. The major benefit of the rolling motion is that it eliminates the tension in the wrist. This tension can cripple pianists by damaging the tendons in the wrist (tendonitis), and must be guarded against constantly. The dropping of the arm produces the good sound; rolling the wrist eliminates tension and is a physical preparation for the second bounce.

Variation C   (Run Mommy, Run Daddy). This variation employs a smaller staccato using some wrist motion. (Very young children may have to use a forearm staccato.)

Theme.   The theme is legato and introduces the pianistic problem of creating the most connected (legato) sound possible between two repeated notes.

Tonalization

Tonalization teaches the first continuous legato playing and should be taught before proceeding further in the repertoire. It is another technique (although it is not designated as such) and is intended to teach legato playing with a beautiful tone. It may be used as a smaller step if a child is having difficulty using legato while simultaneously playing a melody such as *Twinkle Theme.*

Rounded Fingers Versus Flat Fingers

Some teachers have expressed confusion about rounded fingers versus flat fingers. Each is used in a different situation. For rapid passages, rounded fingers are necessary; in slow, melodic, legato playing, the fingers may be less rounded when the wrist is dropped to produce a more beautiful tone. Quite often, a very small child will begin playing with flat fingers. If totally occupied with the playing of the rhythmic pattern Mississippi Hot Dog, the student should not be asked to think about rounded fingers. Later, when the rhythm has been assimilated, rounded fingers may be required. It has been our experience that even very small children can play with rounded fingers, and by the time they reach *Allegretto 2,* their task is made considerably easier if they do play in this manner. We place happy faces on the children's fingernails to encourage them to play with round fingers. (See Chapter 8—*The First Lessons.*)

Technique for the Remainder of Volume One

The *Twinkle Variations* and the five-finger *Tonalization* provide all of the techniques that the children need up to *Short Story* in Volume 2. Since all of the pieces in Volume 1 are to be reviewed constantly, the children have ample opportunity to develop these techniques. When a child has learned Volume 1 completely, we customarily have a graduation party-lesson at which the child plays through the entire volume. At each workshop and recital, one student is especially invited to open the program with a concert performance of the *Twinkle Variations*. This is a special honor, and each child is given both an incentive to practice *Twinkle* and an opportunity to perform it publicly.

The Scale Program

We have developed a method for teaching scales and arpeggios that makes it possible to teach them effectively in a systematic and enjoyable way. This approach helps develop the finger dexterity necessary for performance of the rapid passages in the later volumes and may be started after *Twinkle* and *Tonalization* are well-established. With older beginners, this may occur within six months after the first lesson. Most students are ready to begin scale study when they reach Suzuki Piano Vol. 2. Of course, discretion must be used by the teacher in determining when to begin this part of the student's training; it is impossible to state dogmatically when a student is ready to begin scales. Once the scale program is begun, however, scales must be played at every lesson for it is consistency that yields the best results.

How to Begin: C Major Scale—Hands Separately

1. Discovering the Fingering Pattern.   Point out to the child that the notes to be used are C below Middle C to Middle C for the left hand. There are eight notes, and since we have only five fingers, this presents a fingering problem. If each finger is used once, the teacher and student can determine together how many fingers will have to be used again in order to complete the scale. The teacher, helping the student to reason out loud, may ask which of the five fingers are strongest (1, 2, 3). Since the weak fingers are 4 and 5, it makes sense to use the stronger ones (1, 2, 3) twice. In order for the child to understand the fingering pattern, begin with the left-hand fifth finger on C below Middle C. (Students are used to beginning at this octave from *Twinkle* and many of the other Volume 1 pieces.) The student then plays 5, 4, 3, 2, 1—STOP-PREPARE (no more fingers), puts the third finger over the thumb and plays the remaining notes, 3, 2, 1. The descending scale will use the same pattern in reverse, but the child will need to understand how the thumb tucks under the fingers.

The right-hand scale may be taught in the same manner beginning with the fifth finger on C above Middle C.

2. Thumb Under.   After the child understands the fingering pattern, special attention may be given to the action of the thumb in the ascending right-hand and descending left-hand scale patterns.

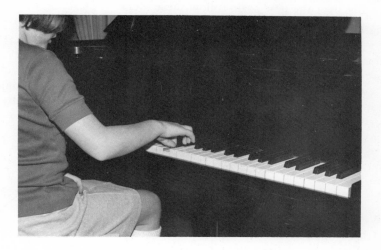

Example of thumb under in scale playing

The following procedure is suggested:

a. Play right-hand thumb—STOP-PREPARE.
b. Second finger is over the next note.
c. When second finger plays, the thumb must tuck under (even though it will not play until after the third finger plays). This is an important preparation for rapid scale playing.
d. Then the third finger plays and is followed by the thumb. Point out the new hand position.

These steps should be practiced many times with each hand.

3. Rhythm.   The one-octave scale is played in a slow quarter-note rhythm and should be practiced hands separately twice each day as the home assignment. The student must count aloud as described on page 105.

4. Technique Portion of the Lesson.   The foregoing introduction to scale playing constitutes the child's first formal technique portion of a lesson. (The teacher should use the phrase "technique part of the lesson" when speaking to the child. See Chapter 5—*Structuring an Effective Lesson*.) If the child is very young or lesson time limited, introduce the above scale program over a two-week period. (First week—left hand; second week—right hand.) Subsequent technique segments will usually take less lesson time.

Continuing the Scale Program

1. Teach one scale per week in quarter notes, hands separately only.
2. Introduce the scales by following the circle of fifths. (C, G, D, A, *etc.*)
3. Discover this week's mystery scale!

   It is possible each week, to make a wonderful game of discovery with the children. Most of them love it so much that they want to spend the whole lesson discovering scale after scale! To discover the new scale follow these steps:

   a. Begin with the current scale, *e.g.,* C Major.
   b. Play the first five notes (counting aloud 1, 2, 3, 4, 5) of the current scale.
   c. Note number 5 is the beginning note of the new scale.
   d. The child is asked to begin playing the old scale (C Major) starting on the new note G, using the C Major fingering pattern.

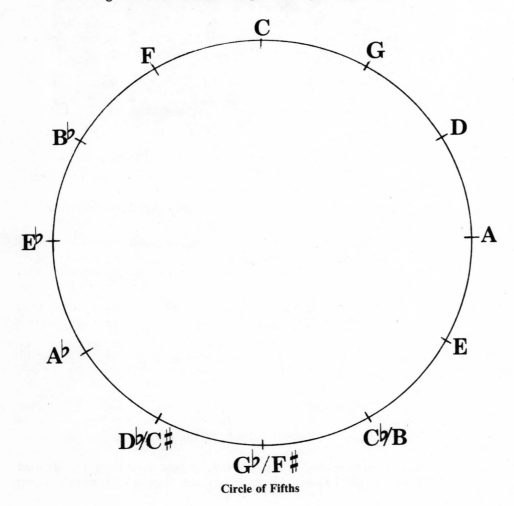

Circle of Fifths

1) The child will hear the wrong note when the seventh degree is played.
2) Allow the child to experiment to correct it.
3) Discovery and Joy! Discuss what happened to make the correction: the seventh degree was raised one semitone.

e. Now there is a new scale and a miracle!

4. Each new scale will have one sharp added to the number of sharps in the current scale. The children learn very quickly that it is the seventh degree that is the new note. This accumulation of sharps continues until the C sharp major scale is reached. The children enjoy noticing that every note of the C sharp Major scale is a sharped note.

5. Change to the flat scales.

a. At this point (C sharp Major scale), the teacher and student can discuss the difference between sharps and flats. From this discussion, the child can easily deduce that C sharp Major may also be thought of as D flat Major. There are only five flats in this scale pattern. From now on, each new scale will be called a flat scale, and since raising a flatted note makes it natural, instead of having one more sharp in the new scale, there will now be one fewer flats. From D flat Major scale with five flats, the new mystery scale, found the same way as before, will be A flat Major with four flats.

$$C\sharp \quad D\sharp \quad E\sharp \quad F\sharp \quad G\sharp \quad A\sharp \quad B\sharp \quad C\sharp$$
$$D\flat \quad E\flat \quad F \quad G\flat \quad A\flat \quad B\flat \quad C \quad D\flat$$

Pattern of Sharps and Flats

6. Scales that use fingering patterns different from C Major.

a. C Major fingering is used for C, G, B, A, and E (B Major used for the right hand only).

b. When the scale begins on a black key, the following rule of scale fingering comes into effect:

1) In the right-hand ascending scale, the thumb must play the first white key.
2) In the left-hand descending scale, the thumb must play the first white key.

c. As a general rule for scale playing, the thumb is never used to play a black key. (Be sure that the student understands that this rule applies *only* to scales.)

d. A memory aid to scale fingering: the fourth finger always plays the same note in a major scale. This helps the student when a finger-crossing decision must be made. (This rule does not apply to several of the melodic minor scales.)

Continuation of Technique

All scales are played *hands separately only*. Evenness of scale work is best developed by playing hands separately. Very few and only very advanced pieces require hands together scale technique. Hands together scale playing will be taught much later and is discussed later in this chapter.

Progression of Scale Teaching

The next step is teaching accented scales of more than one octave. In order to ensure proper accenting, students *must* count aloud. (CAUTION: Do not begin the scale program if a student cannot say aloud a number which does not correspond to the finger he is using. For example, playing the fourth finger while counting the third beat.) The children learn to make an accent with each finger (over the course of the pattern to be described below), and they develop an excellent feeling for a continuous quarter-note pulse, an asset in playing metered scale passages. This is extremely valuable in sight-reading!

1. Teaching Accented Scales.

a. Use $\frac{4}{4}$ meter for all scales, counting aloud and accenting the first beat every time. It is very important that the students count along with the teacher at least in the beginning. It is also a further development of coordination and seems to help establish an inner sense of rhythm and timing.

b. The pattern of the scale requires that the quarter-note establish the beat.

c. The complete pattern is as follows:

One-octave, accented, quarter-note scale.

Two octaves, accented, eighth-note scale, counting 1 and, 2 and, 3 and, 4 and, *etc.* The strongest accent occurs on the first beat with lesser accents on beats 2, 3, and 4.

Three octaves, accented, triplet scale, counting 1 ta ta, 2 ta ta, 3 ta ta, 4 ta ta, *etc.*

Four octaves, accented, sixteenth-note scale, counting 1 ta and ta, 2 ta and ta, 3 ta and ta, 4 ta and ta, *etc.* Strongest accent on the first beat; lesser accents on beats 2, 3, and 4.

2. Sequence of Presentation.

Note: The rhythmic sequence is cumulative, *e.g.,* at Step 4. The student will play 1 octave ascending and descending in quarter notes, followed without pause by the two-octave eighth note pattern, then the triplet pattern, and finally the sixteenth note pattern.

(Hands separately only through Step 4)

STEP	SCALE	PATTERN	EXPLANATION
1.	All Major scales	1-octave	1 octave ascending and descending in quarter notes (see fig. 1)
2.	All Major scales All Harmonic minor scales	2-octave	1 octave ascending and descending in quarter notes (see fig. 1) followed without stopping by 2 octaves ascending and descending in eighth notes (see fig. 2)
3.	All Major scales All Harmonic minor scales All Melodic minor scales	3-octave	1 octave ascending and descending in quarter notes (see fig. 1) followed without stopping by 2 octaves ascending and descending in eighth notes (see fig. 2) followed by 3 octaves ascending and descending in triplets (see fig. 3)
4.	All Major scales All Harmonic minor scales	4-octave	1 octave ascending and descending in quarter notes (see fig. 1) followed without stopping by 2 octaves ascending and descending in eighth notes (see fig. 2) followed by 3 octaves ascending and descending in triplets (see fig. 3) followed without stopping by 4 octaves ascending and descending in sixteenth notes (see fig. 4)
5	Hands Together All Major scales All Harmonic minor scales	4-octave	See above

Arpeggios

After the student has completed the scale program, we introduce a program of arpeggio study that follows the same sequence as the scale program. It is not, however, necessary to begin with one octave. A student who has completed scales in the four-octave pattern is well equipped to manage a four-octave arpeggio pattern and often can play them hands together without special preparation.

Conclusion

Technique, like note-reading, is not dealt with specifically in the Suzuki volumes, but this does not mean that it is to be neglected. It is the teacher's responsibility to ensure that technique is developed in each child. It has been our experience that it is possible to introduce and teach technique with the same kind of step-by-step thoroughness and enthusiasm we use when approaching the Suzuki literature. High spirits and a structured approach are the foundations of a successful technique program. The structure creates the successful experience; the successful experience develops the child's enthusiasm; and the enthusiasm provides the motivation for practicing technique.

Chapter 7
Note Reading

Introduction

"But Can He Read Music?"

Hearing a six-year-old child execute a technically and musically outstanding performance of the Mozart *Piano Sonata in C, K. 545* is an awesome and thrilling experience. This kind of experience, almost unheard of before Talent Education, is commonly tainted with the question: "But can he read music?" It seems immaterial whether or not a child can read if he can play that well. It is, nonetheless, a legitimate question. One of the most frequent complaints about North American Suzuki violin and piano students is that they are not good sight readers; however, this is not a problem unique to Talent Education, because *many non-Suzuki students are not good sight readers either!*

Teaching Note-Reading—the Teacher's Responsibility

A person who can speak his or her language but cannot read it is considered illiterate! If a child is taught to speak with an instrument, but is not taught how to read musical language, the teacher is doing only half the job. The importance of developing music reading is equal to the development of playing ability. It is therefore the responsibility of the Suzuki teacher to make sure that this segment of the child's musical education is not neglected. The Suzuki books do not deal specifically with the teaching of note-reading; consequently, many teachers are not sure when and how to introduce it.

This lack of direction has caused confusion and concern among some Suzuki teachers, and it is hoped that the following suggestions will prove helpful. The two main topics to be discussed are:

1. Note-Reading Materials
2. Procedures for Teaching Note-Reading

In the following section, we wish to make clear that the materials are those which we prefer and have found successful. There are many other note-reading methods for piano and our intention is not to promote or endorse the one we use, but simply to help the novice teacher find a place to begin, or to help the experienced teacher to discover new material. A teacher may apply the procedures which will be discussed to any reading material. It is the teaching procedures that are the vital elements for approaching note-reading, not the materials used.

Note-Reading Materials

The Basic Books

The books we use for teaching note-reading are in a series of four volumes: *The Music Tree,* by Frances Clark and Louise Goss (Summy-Birchard), Volume 1, *Time to Begin,* Volume 2, *Music Tree A,* Volume 3, *Music Tree B,* and Volume 4, *Music Tree C.* We recommend these books for the following reasons:

1. The organization of the material is superb. The presentation follows a logical progression and this orderliness helps children to learn without confusion.

2. The books do not use a Middle C orientation. Many methods introduce reading with five-finger patterns beginning on Middle C. This approach encourages the habit of reading finger numbers rather than the music and often encourages guessing, not understanding. The *Music Tree* student cannot read by numbers because he roams the entire keyboard in the very first exercises. Spanning the keyboard eliminates both the Middle C orientation and the five-finger restriction.

3. Many of the melodies, harmonies, and rhythms are contemporary. This contemporary sound is not only a refreshing contrast to the Suzuki repertoire, but it also broadens the child's musical exposure. In addition, these contemporary pieces prevent aural guessing which is so easy for a Suzuki student with well-developed listening skills.

4. Many of the early tunes have accompanying words which appeal to very young children. In addition to the appeal, the words often describe a mood or picture which the child may try to express in the music. Encouraging expression is an emphasis which is compatible with Suzuki ideals and teaching.

5. The books have music theory exercises at the end of each unit. These exercises, which the children enjoy, visually establish what the child has already learned, and also teach basic music theory.

6. There is no condescension. The presentation is straight-forward and therefore not insulting to a child's intelligence. The ornamental clutter and distracting pictures have been eliminated so that the child is free to concentrate on what needs to be done.

7. The first volume (*Time to Begin*) may be easily understood by a very young child. Television, particularly *Sesame Street,* has contributed to all children's sophistication so that even a four-year old can handle the concepts in this first volume.

8. Each unit contains excellent blank rhythm exercises. These exercises allow the child to concentrate *only* on the rhythm and are compatible with the Suzuki philosophy of dealing with only one problem at a time.

9. Reading is taught by intervals. In our opinion, this is the best way to read music. All musicians read notes by their relationships to each other because reading by letter (subvocalizing) takes too much time.

10. The material cleverly tests the child's understanding. Most children do not like to give wrong answers and expose their lack of knowledge. For this reason, they often pretend to be confused in order to save face. These books are appealing because the testing is subtle. Most children love the challenge which is provided by these books.

Suggested Materials to Follow the Basic Books

A student who has been through the four books of the *Music Tree* will have a basic understanding of reading music and will be able to recognize or analyze any note on the staff or on ledger lines. From this point, he will need only reinforcement of reading skill and exposure to more complex rhythmic problems.

Because the Suzuki repertoire is basically Baroque and Classical, the following two lists of additional material are of contemporary music and technical studies. The lists are in order of difficulty, and it is suggested that the technical studies and contemporary music be alternated to provide the student with more variety.

Contemporary music

1. *Contemporary Piano Literature,* Frances Clark, six volumes (Summy-Birchard).
   These six volumes are in progressive order of difficulty and include short pieces, by several contemporary composers.
2. *Children's Book,* Op 98, Alexander Gretchaninoff (International or Kalmus).
   The level of difficulty in this book is about equal to the Clark, *Contemporary Piano Literature II.* It contains lovely short pieces with descriptive titles which children enjoy interpreting.
3. *Music for Children,* Op. 65, Serge Prokofieff (Kalmus or G. Schirmer).
   This book contains rather difficult selections, but is especially good for reading clef changes and practicing hand crossings.

Technical Studies

1. *A Dozen a Day,* Edna-Mae Burnam (Willis Music Co.).
   Children love these simple exercises and may begin working in the *Dozen a Day, Preparatory Book* when they are at the level of *Music Tree A.* They may then continue with *Dozen a Day, Book One.*
2. *Technic Is Fun,* Volume 1, David Hirschberg (Musichord Publications, Belwin-Mills).
   This series has short pieces that appeal to children. The music in Volume 1 is approximately the same level as *Contemporary Piano Literature, Book 2.*
3. *Selected Piano Studies,* Volume 1, C. Czerny, compiled by H. Germer (Boston Music Co.).
   This book is a compilation of several Czerny works which provides the student with exposure to Czerny without the monotony of learning a great many of the very numerous Czerny studies.

4. *Studies,* Op. 125, Stephen Heller (Kalmus or G. Schirmer).
   This opus is especially good for the teaching of musical expression by reading written markings as opposed to imitating expression from listening. It is also excellent for learning to solve rhythmic problems.

The previous list is only intended to provide help for those who wish to use it and is certainly not meant to eliminate any music or composer. A teacher may choose whatever repertoire the student can understand and execute. The sole purpose of these suggestions is to provide a starting point. There are many excellent sources of repertoire available and since the analysis of all of these volumes would constitute another complete book, this list has been kept brief.

Procedures for Teaching Note-Reading

Whatever method or series of books a teacher uses to introduce note-reading, the teaching procedures, and not the materials, determine the results. The discussion of procedures will include:

1. How to Use the Material.
2. Length of the Reading Assignment.
3. Applying the Suzuki Principles to Note-Reading.

How to Use the Material

First, if a teacher is using the *Music Tree* or any other series it is best to *follow the book carefully in the order given.* Following the order not only gives the child the security of structure, but prevents skipping details that may be important to the child's total understanding of the reading process. Most good methods follow a systematic, step-by-step teaching process, and if skipping around is allowed, the child may become confused and frustrated.

Second, be sure that older students have the benefits of the beginning books. If the teacher is using the *Music Tree,* even *older children should be given the experience of the material in 'Time to Begin.'* Even though this or another similar elementary book seems too easy for the child, the teacher may avoid insult by telling the student it will be easy, and he may move through it as quickly as possible. It will simply be used to guarantee exposure to all of the basic concepts included in this volume.

Length of the Reading Assignment

The *Music Tree* books are organized by units, but *a teacher should not expect to cover one unit per week* because each unit contains a great deal of material. The time restriction must also be considered. The book structure anticipates an entire half-hour lesson per unit, but the Suzuki material must be taught in this time also. Because most of the lesson should be devoted to the Suzuki material, the teacher must budget the time spent on reading. (Suggestions for budgeting lesson time are found in Chapter 5—*Structuring an Effective Lesson.*) If five to ten minutes of every lesson *are spent reading music,* the child will develop reading ability. *Reading at every lesson, no matter how little time is spent,* is what produces students who can read music. Because of the time limit imposed on Suzuki teachers, one will often *cover only one page or even only one piece* during the note-reading segment of the lesson.

Applying the Suzuki Principles to Note-Reading

Dr. Suzuki says, "Each step must by all means be thoroughly mastered." This is interpreted to mean that the student, in addition to mastering the steps in playing, must also master the techniques for note-reading. Teaching note-reading can be combined compatibly with teaching the Suzuki repertoire by the following procedures:

1. **Each new concept must be explained at the lesson.**
2. **Each new song must be played and understood at the lesson.** If this preview does not take place, the child is sent home to learn and not to practice. Practice at home should be used to establish that which the child can already do and should not be a new learning experience.
3. **The note-reading portion of the lesson should deal with only one step at a time.** Many reading lessons cover only one page or even only one song. This is progress! There is no hurry or need to compress everything into one session. If the child masters each step steadily and consistently, progress will be combined with great understanding and security.
4. **The child must perfect each song before going ahead to a new one.** One of the advantages of the Suzuki approach is that the student perfects each piece. This was not always the case in traditional teaching. If a student could manage to play a piece fairly accurately, he was often allowed to move on to a new piece. In applying the Suzuki principles, a teacher should ask that each reading piece be played perfectly and with good musical interpretation. Memorization of the reading material is not required, but it often happens with Suzuki students. They frequently memorize spontaneously, some even memorizing a song after only one playing. This is not a problem, but rather an advantage. Be glad that the memory training is so good. This instant memorization becomes a quick study technique, another benefit of the Suzuki training.

By applying the Suzuki principles of preview, one-step-at-a-time, and mastery, we not only are able to teach reading effectively, but also avoid the following, but common, cycle: The child goes home with a raw assignment which has not been previewed, struggles with practice all week, and learns the piece incorrectly, consequently must spend the next lesson time unlearning these well-established but bad habits. There is no time left to preview the new assignment, so the child goes home with a new raw assignment. And the cycle is repeated!

Conclusion

When Is a Child Able to Read Suzuki Music?

The stage at which a child should be able to read the Suzuki material is impossible to determine because of the many variables. This is much like asking: "When is a child able to read every word he speaks?" Obviously the timing is different for each individual. A few examples and observations derived from experience may help the understanding of how note-reading and note-learning (Suzuki) can work together.

Music reading is a skill quite different from that of playing music by memory, and therefore, reading ability may not always progress as rapidly as playing ability. For example, a child may be playing at the advanced level of Suzuki Volume 4, but may be reading at the elementary level of *Music Tree A*. The most common question is: "Do children object to working at such extremes?" No, the children do not object to playing technically difficult music while reading very elementary music if they understand that the skills are separate and that the reading will progress, too. Reading is treated as a separate skill, and making this distinction clear to the child is usually enough to prevent disinterest in reading. In fact, many students make this distinction themselves by referring to lesson segments as "regular" and "Suzuki"!

A student who completes the *Music Tree A* is probably capable of picking out the right or left hand notes of the Suzuki music if the teacher carefully introduces the intervals and fingerings at the lesson. This is a definite advantage to the child whose parents do not read music because it does not limit the learning of new material to the lesson time.

Many children are able to begin the note-reading program as soon as they can play the *Twinkle Variations* hands together. A student who begins reading this early will very likely be able to read all the Suzuki music at a slow tempo by the time *Music Tree C* is completed and the *Contemporary Piano Literature* is begun. This Suzuki reading obviously will not be true sight reading as the student will be combining aural skills with what he sees on the printed page. The student will probably not be reading the rhythms, as one would do in sight reading, because through listening he already knows how the rhythm should sound. However, the combination of listening and reading will give the child the ability to do a great deal of work independently.

The only true test of reading ability is to have the child read something completely new, as he must then depend totally on reading skills. A child who is playing the Prokofieff, *Music for Children* or the equivalent level, is probably capable of learning the Suzuki music without parental help. Again, these abilities depend on the child. One eight-year-old, who began reading music at age five, was able to read all of her Suzuki music, while another did not reach this level of competence until she was 11. The main factors which determine how well a child reads are: 1) the age of the child, 2) the consistency with which note-reading was taught and reinforced, and 3) the length of time the child has been note-reading (*e.g.*, If the child has been reading for three years, the level will be more advanced than that of the child who has been studying reading for three months.).

Results of the Note-Reading Program

Judging from experience, we have observed that Suzuki students can and do become good sight readers. More significantly, we have discovered that Suzuki students are even better sight readers when compared with traditional students because: 1) they are more sensitive to patterns, both aurally and visually; 2) they pay greater attention to detail on the first reading (*e.g.*, staccato, dynamics, phrasing); and 3) they approach note-reading with confidence. The self-confidence Suzuki students have developed is probably their greatest asset. Confidence creates a positive mental attitude which makes all students more receptive to learning and to new experiences.

Our most exciting observation is that Suzuki students love sight reading. Because they have the confidence and physical skills from their training, and they are following an organized, step-by-step, consistent reading program, they love the challenge of learning a new skill. They do not feel inadequate because their note-reading may not be as advanced as their playing ability. They are simply willing to wait until the skills of playing and reading combine, and they enjoy every step of this learning process.

Chapter 8
The First Lessons

Introduction

Beginnings Are Important

Beginnings are always important and merit special care and consideration. How a task is begun often determines the outcome. A runner who gets a good start will be more likely to win; if a builder prepares a proper foundation, the structure will more likely be sound; and if a student begins study with proper preparation, he will be more likely to succeed. It is therefore necessary for us to deal with the first lessons before analyzing the six volumes of the repertoire.

The Teacher's Preparation

What does a teacher do when the child comes to the lesson for the first time or first few times? (These first lessons are often referred to as "pre-Twinkle" because they involve preparing the child to begin study of the *Twinkle Variations* and the subsequent repertoire.) First lessons are a formidable challenge to the inexperienced Suzuki teacher. The teacher has been immersed in Dr. Suzuki's wonderful philosophy and has been prepared with careful study of the repertoire, but now must deal with a living and often very lively student. There are many ways to approach these exciting first lessons. The suggestions included in this chapter have been developed through our experience and will provide a point of reference from which to begin to apply individual creativity combined with Dr. Suzuki's loving approach to music education.

Children Learn at Different Rates

Because all children are different and each learns at his own individual rate, the suggestions in this chapter are to be used at the teacher's discretion. Everything discussed will be learned eventually, but the teacher must pace it according to the age, maturity, and coordinational development of the child. Perhaps an ability can be learned in a few lessons, and perhaps it will take several months. Obviously a four-year-old cannot absorb as much at one lesson as a nine-year-old. Always remember that it is the development of an ability that is the foremost objective, and not the amount of time it takes for its development.

Pace of Presentation

The first lessons always hold the excitement of a new experience. A teacher must try to generate this excitement and eagerness to learn at every lesson. When the new becomes old, the momentum often slows and motivation can then be difficult. Presenting too many steps before a student has absorbed and mastered each one leads to poor habits and frustration. On the other hand, spending too much time on a single step when the child is well able to move to the next step can lead to boredom and poor habits because the child may not feel challenged enough to concentrate. This judgement, knowing when to remain on the same step and when to proceed, develops with teaching experience and by trial and error.

When dealing with the first lessons, the three main areas are:

1. Preparation for Playing the Piano
2. Playing the Piano
3. Common Problems of Beginning Students

Preparation for Playing the Piano

Preparation for playing the piano will include:

a. The Visual Approach
b. Identification of the Keys
c. Seating the Child at the Piano
d. Posture
e. Introducing the First Rhythm
f. The Correct Hand Position

These preparations may be done in any order the teacher chooses. For young children who cannot concentrate on one idea for more than a few minutes at a time, the teacher may use one idea several different times during a lesson while alternating it with other ideas. For example, the teacher may be working with rhythms and find that the child can no longer concentrate. At this point, another aspect such as key identification should be pursued, followed by a return to the rhythms.

The Visual Approach

When a child enters the room for the first lesson, the easiest way to begin instruction is with the visual approach, that is by *noting the difference between the black and white keys. Point out the black key groupings* and tell the child that they are our friends because they help us to find the correct white keys. (If the teacher covers an area of black keys with a book, the child can easily notice that the white keys all look alike.) Then *ask the child to find all of the groups of two black friends* on the piano. Follow the same procedure for the groups of three. Most children can do this easily; however, if one cannot, help him and proceed without comment to the next idea. The visual relationships will develop in time.

Identification of the Keys

The next step is *teaching the musical alphabet*. This leads ultimately to key identification, and is a *success experience* for the child. Ask the child to recite the alphabet. (Most children can do this without difficulty because of their exposure to television programs such as *Sesame Street*.) When the child reaches G, stop and say that is all that is needed for piano. Marvel at how simple it is. We need to know only seven letters for music as opposed to 26 for reading! Repeat these seven letters several times with the child. Then help him to *play and name all of the white keys on the piano*. The teacher should place the child's index finger on the lowest A on the keyboard as a starting aid. (This help from the teacher ensures success because many children associate the word low with toward the floor and not to their left!)

Once the teacher has helped the child for an octave or two, the child will usually be able to complete successfully the naming process for *all* of the remaining white keys. This key-naming is not necessary knowledge for a beginning Suzuki student at this point, but it is a success experience. Since the student will not have a complete piece to play, this is something that can be done easily and taken home to show to friends and other members of the family. This success experience is worthwhile because it helps the child to build confidence and to reduce apprehension about beginning something new. The child will feel comfortable because he can do something easily and will, therefore, be more relaxed and eager to move to the new steps.

Seating the Child at the Piano

The child is now ready to be seated at the piano. Ask the child to sit facing the *middle of the keyboard*. The teacher should explain how to find the middle by the trademark of the piano. The teacher must also tell the child that there may not be a trademark (many people paint their instruments) and that the foot pedals also indicate where the center is located. When the child is seated with the body centered, show how he can *reach toward the keys at the extreme ends of the keyboard*. Say that because he can reach so far, there is no need to slide on the bench to play the keys near either end. This demonstration will establish a good habit in the beginning, and prevent the sliding so often seen when students have to reach away from the middle of the keyboard.

Once the child is seated and can identify the center of the keyboard, *adjust his height*. Violinists can use smaller or larger violins, but pianists must use an instrument of fixed size and must adjust their height to fit it. It is very important to make this adjustment at every lesson and to *teach the parent* how to do it so that seating at home is also always correct. With the child's hand in the rounded-finger position over the keys, the *forearm should be parallel to the floor*. If the child is seated too high, the wrist and forearm will be too high, and he will not be able to round the fingers or use the relaxed arm weight to produce a good tone; if seated too low, with wrist and palms below the level of the keyboard, the child will play with flat fingers. This is a distorted and crippling position because relaxation

Forearm parallel to the floor

or release of tension from the wrist will be impossible. If an adjustable stool is not available, either at the lesson or at home, the child can be elevated by using firm cushions or a stack of magazines.

After the seat height has been adjusted, the teacher must then be sure that the child's feet are comfortably supported. If the legs are allowed to dangle, the body will be thrown off balance and poor posture habits will result. An adjustable foot stool is best for this purpose, because it tends to be very stable, but if one is not available, a box or a stack of books may be used. One may build or have built a set of graduated footstools, each two to three inches in height, that can be stacked to accommodate any child.

Posture

When the child is seated at the piano with the proper height and feet adjustments, the teacher can discuss posture. When teaching correct posture, the teacher should explain and demonstrate *good body position; the child must be erect but relaxed.* The edge of the bench should touch where the leg joins the body. This is the most comfortable and balanced posture. If too much of the thigh is in contact with the bench, the body's center of gravity is shifted so that support and stability are weakened. The upper part of the body should lean slightly forward to allow maximum freedom of movement. A correctly seated child will be able to raise and lower the arms and lean from side to side freely with the lower part of the body firmly supported. Have the child test the ease and flexibility of this posture.

A teacher should emphasize good posture at every lesson. To establish the habit of good posture, the teacher can ask the child to demonstrate good posture and then say, "I wish I had a camera so that I could take a picture and show everybody how perfectly you sit." By pointing out the positive results, the teacher can make a child conscious of posture without negative statements. If a child does slouch during a lesson, never mention it. Reminding a child of a poor habit simply reinforces it! *To correct posture,* ask the child to stretch his arms in the air, then take hold of the midriff and back, and say, "Now let's play." This will correct posture without calling attention to slouching. A teacher may have to do this several times in a lesson, but by constantly reinforcing good posture, bad habits will be prevented.

Introducing the First Rhythm

Once a child is seated, the teacher can introduce the first rhythm, consisting of four 16th notes followed by two eighth notes. (See Volume 1, *Suzuki Piano School*, p. 10.) The easiest way for a child to understand this rhythm pattern is through the *use of words with corresponding syllables.* We use the words "Mississippi Hot Dog" and will refer to this rhythm as such. Any words the teacher wishes to use are acceptable providing they carry the stress in the proper rhythm. (Examples: Peanut Butter Sandwich, San Francisco Freeway.) It is helpful if the child can *say these words,* so we ask him to repeat "Mississippi Hot Dog" several times. Even more important than speaking the rhythms, however, is having the child feel them. It is easiest to *accomplish this with clapping*. The teacher should clap the rhythm and ask the child to imitate the clapping. This should be repeated many times. The teacher should help any child who cannot grasp the idea at first. The clapping should be continued until the child can do it easily without help. Practicing the clapping can be part of the first week's assignment and the teacher can suggest that the child try to clap along with the recording. The more exactly the rhythm is established, the easier it will be for the child to play.

The Correct Hand Position

The correct hand position should be taught, after the posture and rhythm are established. *Using a tennis ball* is one of the easiest ways to create the correct hand position. Toss or roll the ball to the child (carefully for a young child, because not catching it might be upsetting!). The ball is appealing and helps to relax the child. The teacher can play catch a few times, and then ask the child to hold the ball in the right hand. Ask the child while holding the ball, to turn the hand—palm up, palm down—and repeat this several times. When the child feels at ease, place the hand with the ball over the keyboard (thumb over the C above Middle C). Carefully remove the ball and celebrate the correct hand position!

Celebrate the correct hand position

Playing the Piano

Teaching the child how to play the piano will include:

a. Teaching the Beginning Rhythm (p. 10, Volume 1) Using the Right-Hand Thumb
b. Teaching the Rhythm Using the Remaining Right-Hand Fingers
c. Teaching the Use of the Left Hand
d. Teaching Hands Together

Teaching the above skills will probably require many lessons, but they will all be discussed at this point so that the whole process can be more easily understood. Most children will play several pieces, or at least all of the *Twinkle Variations,* with only the right hand before beginning any left-hand playing at all. Teaching hands together will probably come even later. It is possible for a child to play up to *Little Playmates* or even to the end of Volume 1 with the right hand alone before he is able to begin playing hands together. The teacher must judge when the child is ready to advance to a new skill. Because each child is different, it is impossible to suggest how long it will be before a child is ready to move to a new step.

Teaching the Beginning Rhythm Using the Right-Hand Thumb

Playing "Mississippi Hot Dog" with the right-hand thumb will be the child's first experience at the keyboard. The teacher should first *mark the C above Middle C lightly with a pencil* to help the child identify the beginning key easily. (This octave is used because it allows a more natural position for the child—the body will not interfere with arm movement.) Older beginners sometimes do not need this but having the key marked allows the child to focus his attention on the technique rather than on which key to play. After marking the key, the teacher should then mark the skin on the outside of the right thumbnail with a felt-tipped pen. (See Figure 7, page 153.) This visual aid locates the point at which the thumb contacts the key, and prevents the child from standing the thumb straight on end or from laying it on its side, allowing too much of the thumb to contact the key. Too much thumb contact with the key causes the wrist to fall.

After the key and thumb are marked, the teacher should *grasp the child's hand,* supporting the wrist, and *help him play* "Mississippi Hot Dog". With the teacher guiding the hand, the child can feel the technique. Repeat this step several times, and then ask the *child*

Good right-hand thumb position

to play it alone. If he is successful, *repeat it many times and always STOP after each group to PREPARE* the hand and finger before playing again. This STOP-PREPARE is extremely important and valuable as it sets a habit for all future learning. Stopping to prepare not only ensures that the child will have the proper hand position before beginning to play, but gives the brain time to get the message to the fingers correctly each time. For a detailed discussion of STOP-PREPARE, see Chapter 2—*Preparing to be a Suzuki Teacher.*

The technique involved in the "Mississippi Hot Dog" pattern is *staccato.* The four 16th notes require a wrist staccato with a *small motion staying close to the keys,* and the two eighth notes are played with *either wrist or forearm motion which rises higher from the keys.* With very young children, playing with an arm motion (especially the eighth notes) is often necessary because this coordination uses large muscles and is therefore easier for the child to accomplish. The larger motion will also tend to prevent the slurring of one pattern into the next when the child begins playing consecutive groups of notes. In other words, many children connect the last eighth note of the pattern to the first 16th note of the next. To develop a consistent eighth-note staccato, the teacher can ask the child to practice raising the hand quickly.

The teacher should not be overly concerned if the correct key is not struck cleanly. Aim will improve with practice. The *most important goal should be a relaxed arm and a good arm motion* in order to produce a *beautiful tone. Comparing this technique with baseball* sometimes helps the student understand the lack of concern for the correct notes. A baseball player who is up at bat and uses a poor, stiff form, will only hit foul balls. If his form is correct and he is relaxed, although he may strike out several times, he will ultimately connect with the ball and will very likely hit a home run. When the child can both play the staccato correctly and aim accurately, he can *then try to play several consecutive notes* with the right-hand thumb using the "Mississippi Hot Dog" pattern.

Teaching the Rhythm Using the Remaining Right-Hand Fingers

A child who can play correctly with the right-hand thumb will be ready to play the "Mississippi Hot Dog" rhythm with the remaining right-hand fingers. These remaining fingers *should be taught one at a time following the same procedure used in teaching the thumb.* The fingers are played on five consecutive keys from C to G (See Volume 1, p. 10).

Always STOP-PREPARE after each repetition. When the child can play comfortably and correctly with each finger, he may then try

Good right-hand position

to play the five keys consecutively with STOP-PREPARE after each one. The child should *play with rounded fingers*. However, *many small children have weak fifth fingers,* and these children may rotate the wrist with this finger slightly on the side to gain additional strength from the arm. Avoid allowing the child to use the fifth finger when the hand is completely on the side (thumb pointing up) because this can establish a bad habit.

Teaching the Use of the Left Hand

It is neither necessary nor desirable to begin teaching the left hand before the child is able to play all of the *Twinkle Variations* with the right hand. For children who cannot concentrate well, however, the left hand may be begun sooner. The teacher must decide when to begin work with the left hand. If the child seems ready, *try it,* but if frustration results or the child is unable to manage the coordination, stop the left-hand work for a while and proceed with more right-hand material. Some children play as far as *Little Playmates* or even to the end of Volume 1 before they are ready to work with the left hand. Others may be ready for left-hand work within the first few lessons. The development of coordinational abilities is different for all children.

Teaching the left hand involves the same procedure as teaching the right hand except that the child will begin with the fifth finger on the C below middle C. (See study for Left Hand, Volume 1, p. 10.) Example:

Teaching Hands Together

According to Mrs. Kataoka, at Stevens Point, Wisconsin in July 1978, teaching hands together is not begun until the child plays Cuckoo.

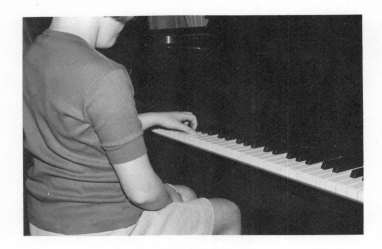

Good left-hand thumb position

(The opening rhythm exercise, Twinkle Variations, Lightly Row, and Honey Bee are taught hands separately only.) If hands-together technique is begun too soon, frustration and poor habits will be the result. If the child cannot manage hands together when it is tried for the first time, move on with right-hand melodies and come back to hands together after the child has developed more ability.

When the child begins hands together, the technique may suffer because he is concentrating only on the coordination. At this point the teacher should overlook the technical problems and work on the development of coordination. Once coordination is no longer a problem, the teacher can remind the child of the technique. The new ability,

Good position—hands together

coordination, will be added to the mastered ability, *technique,* to create a third ability which is the combination of these two. This is much the same as learning to ride a bicycle. At first one must concentrate only on maintaining balance, but once balance is learned, the rider is free to think about where he is going!

Common Problems of Beginning Students

Tension or Rigidity

One of the main problems a teacher encounters in the beginning lessons is tension or rigidity. This is most often caused by fear of failure or concern about playing accurately. To remedy this problem, eliminate the concerns of the child. The teacher can reiterate the baseball analogy (See p. 135) and then work on some physical motions to aid relaxation.

Dusting the keys with a loose wrist is an excellent relaxation motion. The exercise should be done with no attempt to play pitches accurately. Have the child play with this loose feeling, anywhere on the keyboard, using several fingers at once. There should be no thought of controlling even one finger. *To eliminate the tension in the arm, a larger dusting motion* is helpful. Once this looseness is felt, have the child pretend to bounce a ball on the keys. Follow this step with a bouncing motion using only the thumb on one key. This motion can begin small (close to the keys) and gradually grow larger. These types of motions help to relax a child in the early lessons. Once a child gains confidence and feels comfortable, the problems of tension are less likely to occur. Having a child play softly, regardless of level or piece, always promotes relaxation. When the child is trying to make a big sound, he will often feel it necessary to work much harder and tension results. With children, a feeling of lightness is often synonymous with softness. A good general guide to aid relaxation is: the faster the note, the softer the sound or touch.

Low Wrist

Another common problem of beginning students is a low wrist. One possible cause of a low wrist is *improper seating.* The teacher should be sure that the seat adjustment is high enough for the child. If the wrist is still too low, the teacher should check the child's *thumb position.* If too much of the thumb surface is in contact with the key, the wrist will drop. Many children make contact with the key by using the thumb all the way up to the knuckle. To prevent this, the teacher can again mark the skin beside the thumb nail to remind the child to touch the key with that part of the thumb only.

Playing with flat fingers will cause a low wrist and may cause a weak tone. One remedy for this problem is for the teacher or parent to place his or her hand (fingers curved) on the lower ledge of the keyboard just under the child's wrist. The hand is kept on the ledge while the child plays and it acts as a barrier. If the teacher's hand is in the way, the child's wrist cannot drop. In addition, a good visual aid, one that delights small children, is drawing a happy face ☺ on each fingernail except the thumb with a felt-tipped pen. Then ask the child to imagine the happy faces smiling at themselves in an imaginary mirror on the fall board of the piano. If the fingers are flat, the happy faces will look at the ceiling!

High Wrist

Another common problem for beginners is playing with a high wrist. If this happens, the teacher should first check to see that the child is *not seated too high.* If the seating is at the proper height, and the wrist is still too high, one remedy is to ask to see bumps (knuckles) on each finger before it strikes the key. Ask the student to STOP-PREPARE each finger before playing so that he can check for bumps. If the fingers do not have the natural relaxed arch, rigidity will result. Rigidity causes harsh tone. To illustrate the relaxed position, place the child's hand in his lap with the palm up, and have the child relax. The fingers curve naturally in this position. It requires thought to straighten the fingers and this is not natural or relaxed.

Conclusion

In any new experience, excitement is tinged with a certain amount of apprehension. It is during these first lessons that a teacher must capitalize on the excitement and eliminate the apprehension. The fears can easily be erased by the early successes (visual understanding of the keyboard arrangement and identification of the piano's keys). A feeling of success will give the child confidence so that he will approach the other preparations (seating, posture, rhythm, and hand position) with eagerness. After this careful preparation, playing the piano will be a pleasure for the child and paying attention to details (hands separately and hands together with STOP-PREPARE) will be an exciting challenge and not an exercise in perseverance. If a teacher, during these first lessons, prepares the child physically, psychologically, and technically, and is alert to the common problems and their solutions, the student will have the proper foundation to accomplish the forthcoming repertoire with confidence and ease.

Pedagogical Analysis of
Volumes One through Six

of

The Suzuki Piano School

Introduction

Studying Volumes One through Six (Chapters 9 through 14)

In the following analyses we have employed a terse style in outline form which consists of preview material, technical points, and musical points. The purpose of this format is to provide a clear, uncluttered page and consistent form throughout.

The previews, selected as a result of our teaching experience, are the most difficult technical sections of the piece and are placed at the beginning of the analysis; however, they may be taught in several different ways:

1. Some previews are extremely difficult and should be learned several weeks in advance of the new piece being assigned. We have indicated the approximate lead time by suggesting at which prior piece the preview should be started. For example, in Volume 3, the trill preview for the second movement of the Clementi, *Sonatina, Op. 36, No. 3* should be started after the student has learned the Beethoven *Theme* (this is two pieces ahead of the *Sonatina:* the Schumann *Little Rough Rider,* and the Beethoven *Ecossaise,* must still be learned). This information is written on p. 213 with the *Sonatina,* but is meant to be used with the *Theme* on p. 210. To avoid confusion, all information relating to any given piece is kept together. Please read the analysis for several pieces ahead of where the student is.

2. In some cases the pieces divide into clearly defined sections, such as the Mozart *Sonatina* (end of Volume 3, p. 215). All of the previews are listed at the beginning of the analysis, but we generally teach one section at a time in the following way:

   (1) Preview the hard part only for that section (in the *Sonatina* there is no specific hard part in section 1——it is *all* tricky!).
   (2) Learn all of the right hand by memory.
   (3) Play Scramble Game with right hand.
   (4) Learn the left hand in small fragments (not important to memorize, just to feel secure).
   (5) Memorize that fragment hands together.
   (6) Play Scramble Game with the entire section hands together.

   Each of the remaining sections is taught similarly.

3. Some pieces have only one very difficult section. For example, in *A Short Story* by Lichner (Volume 2, p. 179), the piece divides into three sections, with the middle section containing difficult material which is also great fun for the student. We preview and teach the sections in the order 2, 1, and 3.

The technical points in the analyses isolate areas of the music that require particular care in teaching. These sections are not necessarily difficult, but may have unusual fingering patterns, combine contrasting right and left hand techniques or define places where students commonly err. Many of these technical points explain our method of executing the ornamentation. Since this is a subject of great confusion and controversy, we have written out each ornament in rhythm as it is played. Our examples are based on a combination of authenticity, ease of execution, and musicality.

The musical points state our own opinions regarding interpretation. Since no two performances of the same piece are ever exactly alike, the ideas presented here are not intended to represent the only valid interpretation of the repertoire, but to share our ideas and personal feelings about the musical message or mood.

With regards to memorizing each hand separately, we take this position: In most cases, particularly until Volume 4, we have the students memorize the entire right hand. Then we have them learn two or four bar fragments of the left hand and play the two hands together as soon as the student feels comfortable. In the sonatinas especially, the left hands are mostly accompaniment, and since the students are listening to the recordings, they are hearing the complete sound. We can see no reason for making them spend time on something they will never hear that way. The exceptions to this general policy are of course the Bach pieces. The *Minuets* and *Gigue*, for example, at the end of Volume 4, are extremely difficult to play. Each hand of the *Minuets must* be memorized for security. The *Gigue*, however, is impossible to play hands separately because the triplets can be fitted in only with the two hands together; so it seems to us pointless to practice it hands separately. The best way seems to be to play it in one- or two-bar fragments.

The more experience one has in teaching the repertoire, the more successful the results. Since experience is a function of time, study of these analyses will be especially helpful for the novice teacher; however, for all teachers, familiarity with these analyses will be extremely valuable when used as a quick reminder for the key points of each piece.

Chapter 9
Studying Volume One

Introduction

It may be stated unequivocally that Volume 1 is the most important book in the Suzuki piano repertoire. It not only establishes a solid musical and technical foundation for the student, but it also provides a method for approaching, understanding, and executing music that is applicable to all future piano study.

The volume consists mainly of folk tunes arranged for piano. The melodies establish and reinforce legato playing and a feeling for form and musical phrasing. The accompaniments, which often use Alberti basses, prepare the child very well for the performance of music from the Classical Period.

Refer to Chapter 8——*The First Lessons* for pre-Twinkle study. A novice teacher looking at the printed music might be led to believe that the *Twinkle Variations* are to be played hands together almost immediately; however, it is desirable that all the variations be taught hands separately before the child attempts to play hands together. With some children coordination develops at a slower rate. These children should continue to learn right-hand melodies while developing the necessary coordination to play hands together. They may even learn the entire volume of right-hand melodies before playing hands together. Some teachers in Japan do not teach the first three unison pieces in the repertoire (Twinkle Variations, Lightly Row, and Honey Bee) hands together. The first piece the student plays hands together is Cuckoo. The teacher must use discretion in deciding when a particular child is ready to proceed to any new skill, such as hands together technique.

Twinkle Variations —— S. Suzuki

Variation A: "Mississippi Hot Dog"

Preview

1. Refer to Chapter 8——*The First Lessons,* Section B, Playing the Piano.

Technical Points

1. Technique is staccato
   a. Hot Dog——Use a large forearm motion (high bounce)
   b. Mississippi

(1) Play softer than "Hot Dog"
(2) Use smaller arm motion or wrist staccato.
2. First interval (C to G)
   a. Prepare finger position before playing.
   b. STOP after C to PREPARE for G

STOP
PREPARE

N.B. This STOP-PREPARE may be used whenever this interval occurs
throughout the *Twinkle Variations*.

3. Choose fingering of first phrase from:
   a. 1 4 5 4 / 4 3 2 1——right hand
   b. 1 4 5 4 / 3 2 1 1——right hand

Musical Points

1. Strive for good, pleasing tone——avoid harshness
2. Form:
   a. A B B A
   b. Memory aid: describe as a peanut butter and jelly sandwich.
      (1) Bread: First phrase (A)
      (2) Peanut butter: Second phrase (B)
      (3) Jelly: Third phrase (B)
      (4) Bread: Fourth phrase (A)

3. Dynamic contrast between peanut butter (*forte*) and jelly (*piano*).

Variation B: "Bounce Roll Bounce"

This variation introduces the concept of the flexible wrist. We
recommend that all teachers unfamiliar with this concept attend a
workshop to observe a demonstration of this technique.

Preview

The technique for this variation is the preview. Refer to Technical
Points below for teaching.

Technical Points

1. Combines staccato note (Bounce), sustained note (Roll), and
   staccato note (Bounce).
2. The sustained note (Roll) employs the new concept of rolling the
   wrist forward.
3. Teaching the wrist roll:
   a. Mark side of thumb next to the nail with felt-tipped pen. This
      spot is where thumb will contact key. (See Figure 7)

Figure 7

b. Place thumb on key. Tell child that thumb should not slide forward. (It helps if teacher gently holds the child's thumb in position.)

c. With her other hand under the child's wrist, the teacher helps the child move his wrist up and down.
   (1) Child's wrist should be resting on and supported by the teacher's hand.
   (2) Child's elbow follows the wrist forward naturally. (It does not move sideways from the body.)

d. When child can do step c above without the teacher's help, teacher can push the elbow forward to initiate the motion of the wrist.

e. Rolling should be practiced until the child can do it without assistance.
   (1) Some children will manage this technique easily.
   (2) Some children will find this extremely difficult and will take months to master the technique, in which case the teacher may allow the child to continue learning new material while working on the perfection of this technique at every lesson.

4. Playing the "Roll" note.

a. Child drops finger using arm weight to produce a good tone.

b. After the note has been played, the wrist rolls forward.
   (1) This rolling motion releases tension in the wrist.
   (2) This rolling motion lifts the hand and prepares it to play the next note.

5. Playing "Bounce——Roll——Bounce"

a. "Bounce" is staccato.

b. "Roll" is sustained.

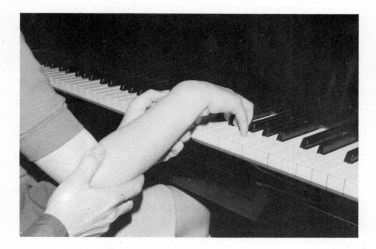

Teacher helping child move wrist

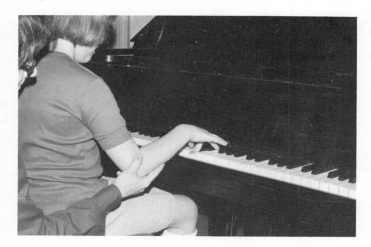

Teacher can push elbow forward

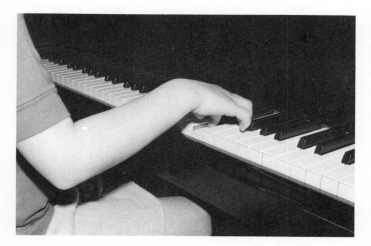

Child can roll wrist without assistance

Musical Points

1. Each "Bounce-Roll-Bounce" pattern must be separated from the next pattern. Children tend to connect the last "Bounce" of a pattern to the first "Bounce" of the next pattern.
   a. Use STOP-PREPARE to prevent slurring of the patterns.

Variation C: "Run Mommy, Run Daddy"

Preview

None. Most children can do this variation easily.

Technical Points

1. Encourage playing this with rounded fingers.
2. Technique is staccato.

   a. Very young children may use small arm motion.
   b. Some children may be able to produce a wrist staccato.

Musical Points

1. Each "Run Mommy, Run Daddy" pattern must be separated from the next pattern. Children sometimes link these patterns when changing to the next finger.
   a. Use STOP-PREPARE to prevent slurring of the patterns.

2. It is desirable to use a softer tone than was used in *Variation A* because of the wrist staccato.

Variation D: Twinkle Theme

Preview

None

Technical Points

1. The technique is legato.
   a. A helpful image for children: Imagine fingers are sticky.
   b. Strive for the most connected sound possible between repeated notes.
   c. Rolling the wrist and maintaining the sound until the last possible instant assists the child with the creation of a beautiful legato.

Musical Points

1. Should be played with a relaxed arm so that the piano will sing.
   a. Compare tone to a voice that has no spaces between the sounds except to take a breath (phrase ending).
2. Strive for as big a sound as the child can produce without harshness.
   a. Encourage the child to listen to each piano's unique sound and to try to hear when the piano stops singing and begins to shout.

Tonalization

This is an expansion of and reinforcement for legato playing.

1. Allows the child to concentrate only on the connection of the notes without the additional task of remembering a melody.
2. Is a valuable technical exercise and should be reviewed as regularly as the *Twinkle Variations.*
3. May be used to develop the flexibility of the wrist.
   a. Child rolls wrist on every note.
4. Useful as a preparation for finger action (without rolling wrist) in later repertoire (*e.g., Little Playmates*).
5. Practice hands separately; then hands together when child develops this ability.

Lightly Row —— Folk Song

Preview

1. The first phrase. Skipping fingers is new coordination.

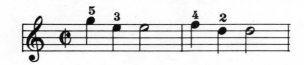

Child rolling wrist for beautiful legato

Tonalization—example of rolling wrist on every note

Technical Points

1. Memory aid: Scramble Game (See Chapter 4——*Motivating Students* for description of benefits and use.)
2. Develops legato technique.
3. New technique is skipping fingers. See Preview above.

Musical Points

1. Further develops legato concept and beautiful tone of *Twinkle Theme*.
2. Roll wrist on repeated notes and half notes to sustain.

The Honeybee —— Folk Song

Preview

1. Fingering sequence:

Technical Points

1. Encourage rounded fingers for good finger action. (Very young children may not be able to do this.)
2. Roll wrist only on half notes.

Musical Points

1. First piece with rests.
   a. We tell children that when Mozart was asked which was the most beautiful music, he said, "No music," meaning the rests between the notes. Ask children to listen for this beauty.

Cuckoo —— Folk Song

By the time the child can do *Honeybee* well hands together, he has probably known the right hand of *Cuckoo* for some time. If the teacher chooses not to have students play unison pieces hands together, the right hand must be secure before the left hand is taught.

Preview

1. Teach hands separately. This should be secure before teaching hands together.
2. First Measure——hands together.
   a. Use STOP-PREPARE

Technical Points

1. Scramble Game helps learning, both hands separately and hands together.
2. First piece using different left hand——new technique.
3. Establish hands together securely before attempting *Lightly Row* with Alberti Bass hands together. (Children tend to confuse the two left-hand patterns.)

Musical Points

1. Strive for singing tone with beautifully shaped phrases.

Lightly Row ——with Alberti Bass —— Folk Song

This is by far the most difficult ·coordination challenge the child has yet attempted. Some children find it very difficult so preview this carefully.

Preview

1. Left hand Alberti Bass figure.
2. Hands together——first measure.
   a. Use STOP-PREPARE so that child does not lift left hand when right hand lifts for repeated note.

Technical Points

1. Alberti Bass is the new technique.
    a. Establish well——it occurs in many subsequent songs.

Musical Points

1. Phrases can be shaped musically.
    a. Wait until hands together technique is secure before introducing phrase shaping.

French Children's Song —— Folk Song

Preview

1. Teach entire right hand first.

Technical Points

1. First two phrases hands together do not usually present a problem.
2. Third phrase is difficult.
    a. Be prepared to spend time here.
    b. Use STOP-PREPARE after each measure.

    c. Memory aid: Note where second and fourth fingers of each hand play together.
3. Scramble Game especially helpful.
4. Left hand plays in the Middle C octave for the first time.
    a. Be sure child is not seated too close to piano; body may interfere with elbow.

Musical Points

1. Strive for beautiful tone and legato with shaped phrasing.

London Bridge —— Folk Song

Preview

1. Learn entire right hand first.
2. First measure——hands together.
    a. Use STOP-PREPARE

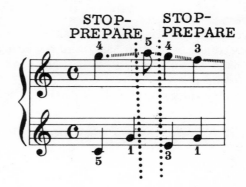

Technical Points

1. Alternate fingering for the last two measures.
   a. Use STOP-PREPARE.

   b. If printed fingering is used——STOP-PREPARE at end of previous measure.

Musical Points

1. Smooth phrasing for dotted rhythm.

Mary Had a Little Lamb —— Folk Song

Preview

1. Learn entire right hand first.
2. Left hand chords.

Technical Points

1. STOP-PREPARE at end of each measure for left hand lift and right hand legato.

Musical Points

1. A good piece to introduce concept of balance between hands.
    a. Practice beginning with right hand third finger high above keys and left hand chord close to keys. (right hand——*forte;* left hand——*piano.*)
2. Right hand is played legato throughout.

Go Tell Aunt Rhody —— Folk Song

Preview

1. Learn entire right hand first.
    a. Use STOP-PREPARE for hand position change at end of second phrase.

2. Left hand subdominant harmony in Alberti Bass figure (third phrase).

Technical Points

1. Requires same technique as *Lightly Row* with Alberti Bass.
    a. Use STOP-PREPARE so that child does not lift left hand when right hand lifts for repeated notes.

Musical Points

1. Develops beautiful tone and phrasing.

Clair de Lune —— J. B. Lully

Preview

1. Learn entire right hand first.
    a. STOP-PREPARE for hand position change at end of second phrase.

Technical Points

We have found it easiest to teach this piece using the following procedure:

1. Teach first two measures of left hand.
2. Play first two measures hands together.
3. STOP-PREPARE: Child may now play measures three and four hands together. (Motion is parallel——this is usually easy for children to grasp.)

4. Teach the difference between the endings of the first and second phrases in the left hand.
5. Teach third phrase hands together, one measure at a time.
6. Last phrase——hands together
   a. First two notes——like beginning.
   b. STOP-PREPARE: Remainder of piece moves in parallel motion.

Musical Points

1. Beautiful tone and shaped phrasing.

Long, Long Ago —— *T. H. Bayly*

Preview

1. Third phrase (third line), first two measures for smooth interval of the seventh.

2. Teach entire right hand.
   a. Note right-hand finger change on repeated note.

Technical Points

1. Measure three, left hand——note chord change.

Musical Points

1. Beautiful tone and legato melody.
2. Suggest an echo effect in the third phrase.

Little Playmates —— *F. X. Chwatal*

Preview

1. Teach the following pattern for the right and left hands—— separately.

   a. Encourage rounded fingers for articulation.
   b. Rhythm is the same as Mississippi Hot Dog. (High bounce on Hot Dog.)

   Technical Points

1. First piece to give feeling of speed.
2. STOP-PREPARE to lift left hand chord and sustain right hand melody each time this occurs.

   Musical Points

1. First piece to indicate dynamics.

Chant Arabe ——— Anonymous

   Preview

1. Teach first two lines of right hand.
2. Demonstrate left hand fifth:
   a. Many students can now play these two lines hands together.
   b. For students who have difficulty, use STOP-PREPARE technique similar to that of *London Bridge*.

   Technical Points

1. Teach last two lines in four segments of two measures each, right hand only.
   a. Note: First and third segments are identical.
   b. It is desirable for child to learn to play this without looking at the keyboard, so that he can watch the octave leap in the left hand when played hands together.
2. Last two lines——left hand.
   a. Octave leap is a new technique.
   b. Once octave leap is secure, teach hands together in two measure segments.

c. Children with small hands should be taught to watch the left
hand for accuracy of octave leap.

Musical Points

1. Phrase melodic sequences consistently.
2. Encourage balancing of melody and accompaniment.
   a. Aid for teaching left hand control: Have child try to play left
   hand silently. (Easiest on first two lines.)

Allegretto 1 —— C. Czerny

Preview

1. Left hand: New dominant seventh chord and position change as
follows:

2. Learn entire right hand.

Technical Points

1. Review *Cuckoo;* with this preparation, some students can learn
this entire piece hands together at one lesson.

Musical Points

1. Beautiful phrasing. Do not accent thumb.
2. Note dynamic contrasts.

Adieu! —— Folk Song

Preview

1. Teach entire right hand first.
   a. Memory aid: Every phrase except one begins with the third finger on B.

Technical Points

1. Once the right hand is learned, most children find it easy to play this piece hands together without having to memorize the entire left hand alone.
   a. Teach and establish first two beats hands together.

   b. Second line contrary motion hands together is easy to grasp once the child is shown the left hand notes; teach left hand notes in two-measure segments.

Musical Points

1. Most children enjoy playing this piece with a *diminuendo* and *rallentando* at the end.

Allegretto 2 —— C. Czerny

Previews

None. Most children learn this totally by ear before they ever get to it.

Technical Points

1. Be sure right and left hand notes sound simultaneously.
   a. Practice measure one to establish this technique.

2. Establish last two measures hands together; lively tempo makes combining consecutive motion and skipping intervals difficult.

3. For clarity and speed, encourage rounded fingers.

Musical Points

1. First piece using strong accents.
2. Use a light touch and softer dynamics to produce a crisp staccato and make playing faster, easier.

Christmas-Day Secrets —— T. Dutton

Preview

1. Right hand——first line.
2. Left hand——first line.
3. First measure——hands together.
   a. Right hand: Roll-Lift.
   b. Left hand: Legato.

4. Measure two——hands together.
   a. Mississippi Hot Dog rhythm: Eighth notes are staccato in contrast to the rolled eighth notes in the first measure.
   b. Right hand: For control, encourage rounded fingers on 16th notes. This promotes an even sound when played with the left hand.

Technical Points

1. Lines three and four (very difficult).
    a. Teach hands separately in two-measure segments.
       (1) Note: First and third segments are identical.
    b. STOP-PREPARE for position changes in right hand and left hand.
    c. Introduce new skills:
       (1) Left hand: Thumb under.
       (2) Left hand: First black key.
    d. Teach hands together in two-measure segments.

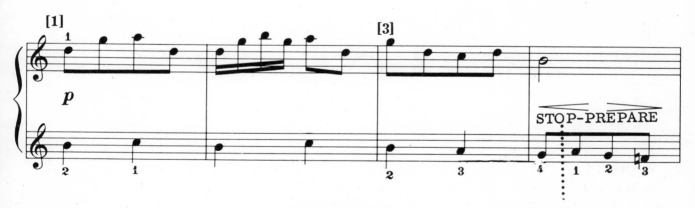

Musical Points

1. Bring out the different touches to add greatly to the charm of this piece.

Allegro —— S. Suzuki

Preview

1. First line——right hand.
    a. High bounce for all staccato quarter notes.
    b. Measure two.

(1) STOP-PREPARE at beginning to place the third, fourth, and fifth fingers deep into the keyboard so that the fourth finger can play the black key (F sharp) without distorting the hand position.

(2) Eighth notes use finger staccato and hand stays close to the keys.

2. First line——left hand.

    a. Take special care when changing from G chord to D chord.

        (1) Hand must go deep into keyboard so that fifth finger can play F sharp without distorting arm position. Hand must come out again for next chord.

Technical Points

1. Playing hands together.

    a. Right hand bounces high and plays *forte*.

    b. Left hand stays close to the keys and plays *piano*.

Musical Points

1. Strong contrasts between staccato and legato sounds.
2. *Dolce* (middle line) slows the tempo *very* slightly, guard against dragging.
3. Observe *rit.* and *fermata*.

Musette —— Anonymous

Preview

1. Teach right hand——first line.
2. Teach left hand——first line.

    a. Prepare for thumb on black key (B flat). The second finger may be described as walking toward the black key.

Technical Points

1. Middle line——difficult.

    a. Learn well hands separately.

    b. Observe left hand fingering carefully.

    c. Teach hands together in two-measure segments.

    d. Second phrase.

        (1) STOP-PREPARE after each note in playing hands together to ensure right hand legato.

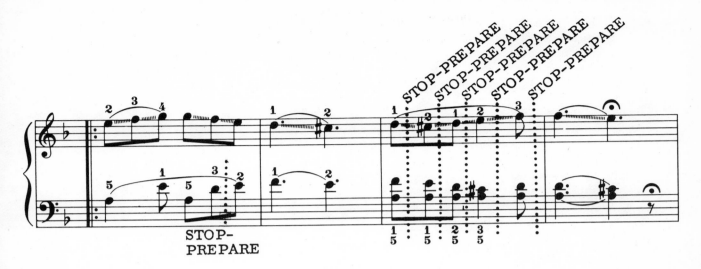

STOP-
PREPARE

Musical Points

1. Phrases may be described as arches of sound.
   a. The fifth finger plays loudest in the first phrase because the A is the peak of the arch.

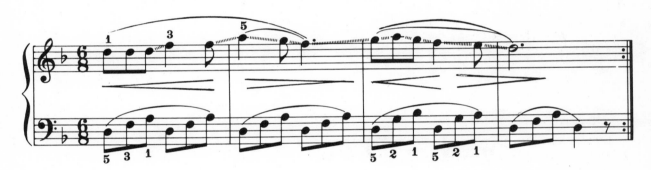

2. Note: Cadences, second line——second and fourth measures.
   a. Tension and repose expressed through dynamics (loud to soft).

Chapter 10
Studying Volume Two

Introduction

Volume 2, in comparison to Volume 1, is noticeably more difficult. It is wise to prepare the child psychologically for this change because he is used to learning entire pieces quickly and now will likely need several weeks for each one.

Careful previewing is critical in Volume 2. The child is moving from folk tunes to major piano repertoire. The pieces have been written especially for the piano by composers.

Ecossaise —— J. N. Hummel

Preview

1. First two bars——right-hand arpeggio.

2. Grace-note measure.

3. Left hand (second half). This is a new technique——holding the bottom note with a moving inner voice. STOP-PREPARE at the end of each measure by holding thumb note while preparing the new hand position. It is not necessary for children with small hands to hold the thumb note during STOP-PREPARE.

Technical Points

1. Practice the first measure hands together with careful attention to legato in right hand and lifting in left hand. (There is a tendency to lift both hands and develop an uneven rhythm.)

2. Use STOP-PREPARE for fingering in third measure.

Musical Points

1. A very sturdy piece with marked dynamic contrasts.

A Short Story ——— H. Lichner

Preview

We teach this piece in three sections using the following order:
1. Second section (Left hand ascending scale passages).
   a. Left-hand scales.
   b. Right-hand double thirds and double sixths.

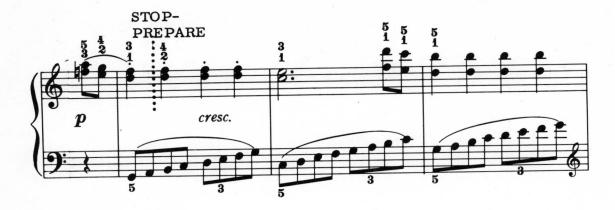

c. Hands together before proceeding.
   (1) Use STOP-PREPARE for the ending of this section.

2. First section.
   a. Hands separately.
      (1) Practice left-hand leap as blocked chord first, then as written.
   b. Use STOP-PREPARE for right-hand fingering.

c. Hands together.
   (1) Use STOP-PREPARE for contrary motion leap.

STOP-
PREPARE

3. Third section.
    a. Right hand.
    b. Left-hand chords.

    c. Left-hand descending scale.
    d. Hands together.

Technical Points

1. Practice right-hand double thirds without watching keyboard so that eyes are free to find the left-hand leap.
2. Practice left-hand "flying" from high to low notes in scale passage.

3. This piece combines melody and accompaniment plus scale passages and chords.

Musical Points

1. This is the first lyrical piece with graduated dynamics.

The Happy Farmer —— R. Schumann

Preview

1. Left-hand first line.
2. Right-hand first line.

    a. Note correct fingerings.
    b. Observe quarter-note chords.
3. Hands together first line.

Technical Points

1. Right hand——leap from C to B flat is difficult.
2. Note where left hand plays B flat in the same measure.

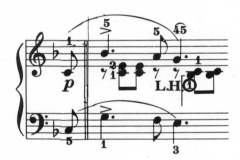

Musical Points

1. First piece with the melody in the left hand.
    a. Listen for balance; left hand must sing; right hand plays softly.
2. Left-hand upbeat softer than following downbeat in each phrase.

Minuet 1 —— J. S. Bach

    This is the introduction to Baroque counterpoint. Prepare the child psychologically for spending a long time on these Bach minuets. They are not easy to learn and memorize. Their accomplishment should be enthusiastically rewarded.

    There is some controversy about whether the student should memorize the minuets hands separately. We feel that the students should be allowed to play hands together as soon as they can comfortably do so because of the intensive listening they have done.

Preview

1. Memorize entire right hand. (One phrase or less at a time.)

2. Teach left hand in segments.
3. Play hands together as each left-hand segment becomes secure.
   a. For many students it is not necessary to memorize the entire left hand before attempting segments hands together.

Technical Points

1. We do not make an issue of holding the dotted half note for the entire second measure (left hand) or other similar measures.

2. The repeated notes in the first measure are not staccato; they are played with a good tone and as legato as possible.

Allegretto

3. Observe fingerings carefully.

Musical Points

1. By the time students reach this piece they have developed a beautiful legato and are able to phrase sensitively.
2. Observe where there is a phrase continuation in one hand and a phrase ending in the other.

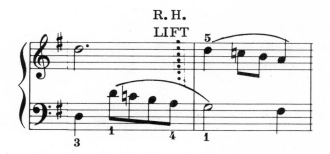

Minuet 2 —— J. S. Bach

The most difficult and rewarding piece in Volume 2. Begin preview while child is polishing *The Happy Farmer*.

Preview

1. Right hand——first two measures. Break into three parts:
   a. Four-note arpeggio——prepare third finger on D before starting.

b. Practice A, F sharp, G, creating the biggest sound with the smallest finger (5).

c. Repeated G with thumb——very lightly with wrist roll on each note to prevent sharp staccato.

2. Left hand arpeggio——fourth finger on B is essential.

3. Play these first two measures hands together before learning any other part hands separately. (Prepare both hands on D before beginning to play.)

4. Left hand——B major arpeggio (in second half of piece)——note fingering.

5. Memorize remainder of right hand; learn left hand in segments; play hands together as each left hand segment becomes secure.

Technical Points

1. Play triplets carefully, connecting fifth finger to thumb.

2. Note the following example; use STOP-PREPARE for leap.

3. Note the following example; use STOP-PREPARE:
   a. Right hand stretches for E.
   b. Left hand squeezes for G.

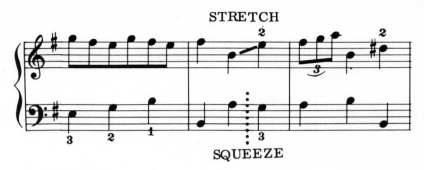

Musical Points

1. This is a most exuberant minuet. The possibilities for musical phrasing and dynamic shadings are endless.

Minuet 3 —— J. S. Bach

Preview

1. Memorize entire right hand. (One phrase or less at a time.)
2. Teach left hand in segments.
3. Play hands together as each left-hand segment becomes secure.

Technical Points

1. Emphasize the quarter note in the following pattern:

a. The quarter note must sing. The eighth notes are softer.
b. This rhythmic pattern occurs a total of 15 times in each hand. Students enjoy noticing how the repetition of this simple pattern creates a masterpiece.
2. Note the following example:

Printed: Played:

a. The small note is **not** a grace note or *acciaccatura* (♪), but is an *appoggiatura* (♪) which is played on the beat. It is a full eighth-note, and takes its time from the note that follows it, the dotted half note.

3. Use STOP-PREPARE for the following interval hands together.
   (After double bar.)

Musical Points

1. For beauty of counterpoint, phrase carefully and note continuation of phrasing in left hand while the right hand phrase ends, as in the following example:

Minuet in G Minor —— J. S. Bach

This lovely piece is easy to learn, and many children can play through it hands separately at one lesson and often return to the next lesson playing it hands together.

Preview

1. Memorize entire right hand (One phrase or less at a time).
2. Teach left hand in segments.
3. Play hands together as each left-hand segment becomes secure.

Technical Points

1. First piece with two flats.
   a. Try to play black keys with rounded fingers.
2. Observe all fingerings carefully, especially in the following difficult passage:

Musical Points

1. Beautiful melodic counterpoint. An excellent example for tonalization. We tell the children that if they play this piece with love, the piano will sing for them.
2. Play repeated B flats as connectedly as possible, observing fingering.

Cradle Song —— C. M. von Weber

Preview

1. Teach entire right hand——one line at a time. (Number the lines and use Scramble Game.)
2. Teach left hand one line at a time.
   a. Play hands together as soon as each left hand line is learned.

Technical Points

1. For ease of execution, the 16th notes on the first line should be played softly.

2. Encourage balancing the melody with the accompaniment.
   a. An aid to controlling the left hand: Have the student play the left hand notes silently while playing the right hand loudly.
   b. When the student can play the left hand silently, and the right hand loudly, he may then attempt to sound the left hand, balancing the melody with the accompaniment.

Musical Points

1. The homophonic style contrasts with the Baroque.
2. Beautiful phrasing is essential.
3. *Cantabile* implies at least a *mezzo forte* for the right hand melody.

Minuet in F —— W. A. Mozart

Preview

1. Right hand——Teach first measure rhythm, accents, and light thumb.
   a. The accent must fall on the first beat, contrary to the natural tendency to accent the quarter notes.

2. Memorize entire right hand (one phrase or less at a time).
3. Teach left hand in segments.
4. Play hands together as each left-hand segment becomes secure.

Technical Points

1. Repeated notes (Bar one and similar measures) must be played lightly and as connectedly as possible.
2. All cadences must be played loud to soft. Saying the word "Mozart" helps the students to remember.

Musical Points

1. Singing tone in the right hand creates a beautiful, lilting melody which is connected in feeling despite the repeated thumb on the second and third beats.
2. Students enjoy the humor of the deceptive cadence which then relaxes at the conclusion with a perfect cadence.

Deceptive
Cadence

Arietta —— W. A. Mozart

Preview

Begin after right hand of Mozart *Minuet* is memorized.

1. Right-hand dotted rhythms——use STOP-PREPARE after each
   dotted note. We have found it best to teach only one of the dotted
   rhythm measures per week.
   a. Teach right hand first.
   b. When right hand is secure, preview hands together.

2. Teach right hand to double bar.
3. Teach left hand to double bar.
   a. First note of each measure is sustained and connected to the
      first note of the next measure, creating a legato line.
   b. Thumb must be played evenly, lightly, and detached.

4. Teach hands together to double bar.
5. Teach remaining right hand.
6. The following passage is difficult:
   a. Left hand——first note of each measure is sustained and connected to the first note of the next measure, creating a descending, legato line, except where fifth finger must move to play again.
      (1) Take special care with the fingering.
   b. Right hand——Use STOP-PREPARE.

Technical Points

1. After double bar, right hand bounces high and left hand stays close to keys for forte and balance. When this figure repeats, right hand stays close to keys for piano.
2. Whenever melody has three repeated, staccato eighth notes, be sure last eighth note is staccato.

Musical Points

1. This is a little aria and should be played as if sung by a beautiful voice.
2. In the measure before *leggerio,* think of increasing volume to the F, which acts like a springboard for the light *coloratura* sound of the *leggerio.*

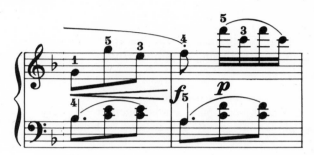

"Melody" from Album for the Young ——
R. Schumann

Preview

1. Use first line as tonalization (use score for correct fingering and notation instead of printed tonalization).

Andante

p dolce

2. Finger substitution measures——right hand.
   a. This is the most difficult measure of the entire piece and must be taught with care.
   (1) Observe fingering.
   (2) Hold dotted quarter note (F) for full value to maintain legato for the entire phrase.
   (3) Last note of measure (D)——roll wrist forward to prepare fingers ($^5_2$) for the next measure.

ROLL WRIST
FORWARD

b. This is easy after the first finger-substitution measure, but must be carefully fingered.

3. Memorize hands separately, one line at a time.
4. Play hands together using Scramble Game.

Technical Points

1. Balance between hands is important.
   a. When student can play hands together securely, have the left hand played silently to aid learning of balance.

Musical Points

1. The phrases of this elegant melody should be shaded beautifully.

Sonatina in G —— L. van Beethoven

Moderato

Preview

1. Two-note phrases in the right hand. Saying "Down-Up" for each slur helps students execute this technique.

   a. Observe fingering carefully in each two-note phrase.
2. First three left hand chords. Place hand deep into keyboard (fingers close to the black keys), so that the fifth finger can reach F sharp more easily.

3. Introduction of *portato* in left hand.

4. Teach entire right hand, observing fingerings carefully.
5. Teach left hand in segments. Play hands together as soon as left hand is secure.

Technical Points

1. The grace note (*acciaccatura*) is played before the beat.
2. Play the right hand half-notes firmly so that their tone will last for the full value; the eighth notes by comparison are played much softer.

Musical Points

1. Observe contrasting and graduated dynamics.
2. Pay careful attention to the left hand rests which add character.

Romance (Allegretto)

Preview

1. Teach right hand to double bar, carefully observe phrasing and fingering.
2. Teach left hand to double bar; note with care marked slurring, phrasing, and sustained notes.
3. Play hands together to double bar.

Romance

4. Middle section——left-hand rolled chords.
   a. Be sure right-hand fifth finger sounds with left-hand thumb. (Other left-hand notes precede.)

Printed: Played:

    b. Carefully observe right-hand slurring which precedes rolled chord.

Technical Points

1. Middle section——for student who cannot span an octave, play upper bass staff note (D) with right hand. Finger $\frac{4}{2}$ with right hand.

2. Note suggested phrasing in the following example and carefully observe staccato markings.

3. Ornaments in final section.
    a. Ornament is played on the beat, and measure should be played in strict time.

    b. The following ornament is a grace note and should be played ahead of the beat.

Musical Points

1. Light, happy, lilting interpretation.
2. Observe contrasting and graduated dynamics.

Sonatina —— W. A. Mozart

For those who have the old books: although this piece is printed here, it should not be taught until the end of Volume 3. It has been correctly placed in the newer editions, and will therefore be discussed in the new position. See page 136.

We suggest that the study of the following two pieces be delayed until the Clementi, *Sonatina, Op. 36, No. 1* found in Volume 3 has been mastered.

"Musette" from English Suite III in G Minor —— *J. S. Bach*

Preview

1. Teach entire right hand phrase by phrase. Play Scramble Game for security.
2. Teach left hand one phrase at a time, playing hands together as soon as secure.

Technical Points

1. New technique——holding down fifth finger of left hand (expanded from *Ecossaise*).
2. Right hand must phrase while left hand continues without interruption. (Use STOP-PREPARE for right hand lift.)

Tempo di Gavotta

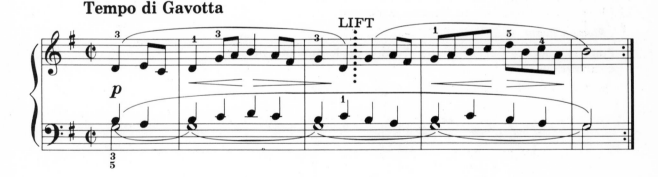

Musical Points

1. A musette is a bagpipe song and the left-hand fifth finger represents the drone of the instrument.
2. Careful phrasing and dynamic shading will bring out the beauty of this piece.
3. Last phrase:
   a. Lift right hand slightly between each group of four eighth notes.
   b. The last left hand tied G may be struck again. After a long tie this creates a better ending.

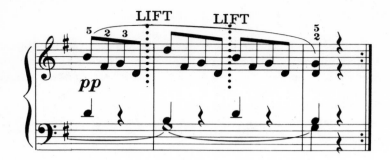

Minuet in G Minor —— J. S. Bach

Preview

1. The following right-hand passage from the last line.

2. Teach entire right hand. (One phrase or less at a time.)
3. Teach left hand in segments.
4. Play hands together as each left-hand segment becomes secure.

Technical Points

1. Not difficult to play, but difficult to memorize hands together.
2. Use a *portato* touch where staccato is indicated.

Musical Points

1. Practice cadences carefully for beauty of legato and *portato* combination.

2. This is similar in style to Minuet 3 and may be played in combination with Minuet 3 in the following order:
   a. Minuet 3 with repeats.
   b. Minuet in g minor with repeats.
   c. Minuet 3 without repeats.

Chapter 11
Studying Volume Three

Volume 3 introduces the student to the Classical sonatina. The students not only enjoy learning these sonatinas and take pleasure in playing this repertoire, but they also develop the ability to concentrate on longer pieces and build the technical foundation for the major Classical sonatas in the later volumes.

Sonatina, Op. 36, No. 1 —— M. Clementi

Allegro

Preview

1. Broken double third passage (Measures 6-7)——Note fingering. Right hand.

2. Rotary octaves (after double bar).
    a. This is a difficult new technique.
    b. Students with small hands must be able to play the left hand without looking so that they are free to watch the right hand play the octaves.

etc.

Technical Points

1. Playing scales evenly is important.
   a. Careful fingering is mandatory.
   b. Rounded fingers are essential.
2. Practice opening Cs in both hands.
   a. For balance play left hand *piano,* right hand *forte.*
   b. Establish different touches (Begin right hand high and left hand close to key).
   c. Both hands roll wrists (Left hand note has tenuto mark).

Musical Points

1. Strong dynamic contrasts give vigor to this movement.
2. Measure two, beat four: Play as marked——The G is slightly detached from the following run.

Andante

Preview

1. Trills.
   a. This is a new technique.
   b. Play four notes for each left-hand note, begin on upper auxiliary.
   c. All three trills use the same formula.
   d. Preview the trills when student begins first movement.

2. Right hand——Double thirds.

a. Must be played simultaneously.

b. Bring out the upper note, if the student is able to do so.

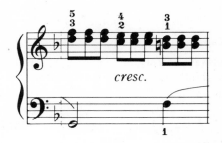

Technical Points

1. Melody should sing above the accompaniment.
2. Memory aid: Line four, right hand begins on C alone——left hand enters on C; the next right-hand phrase begins on B flat——left hand enters on B flat.

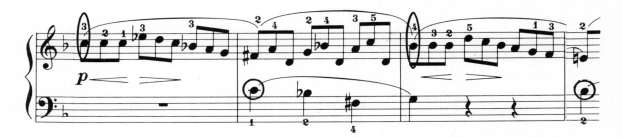

Musical Points

1. Melody must flow smoothly.
2. Half notes must sing with a beautiful tone; balance by playing quarter notes softer.

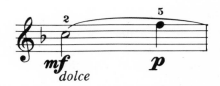

3. Observe the phrasing in Measure 17. Lifting the hand suggests breathing.

Vivace

Preview

None. If the student has had the cumulative experience of listening and has mastered the first movement, this will be easy.

Technical Points

1. Play scale passages evenly.
2. Play left hand lightly (especially the chords).

3. Opening measure and similar measures: Accent must fall on the first note.

Vivace

Musical Points

1. This is a light, happy movement.
2. Children like to play it fast.
3. Dynamic contrasts give this movement sparkle.

We suggest that the Bach *Musette* and the Bach *Minuet in g minor* in Volume 2 be studied at this time. See page 123-24 for preview, technical points, and musical points.

Sonatina, Op. 55, No. 1 —— Fr. Kuhlau

Allegro

Preview

1. Syncopated phrases. (Where accents occur on weak beats).
   a. Measures seven and eight. (It is helpful for the student to say "drop-lift").

b. Measures 18 through 20:
   (1) Left hand observes the phrasing.
   (2) Right hand plays *all* legato. (No lifts until the repeated note.)

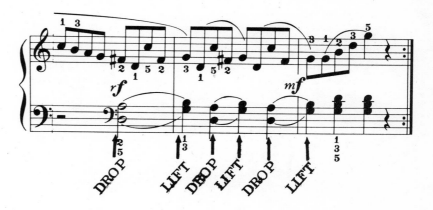

2. Measures 37 and 38——right hand: Preview fingering carefully.

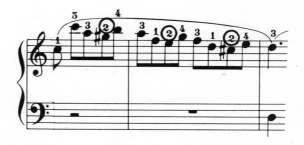

3. Measures 47 through 49——left hand: Octave stretch in the Alberti Bass figure is difficult for students with small hands.

Technical Points

1. At this level of advancement, student should strive for lighter and more even left hand ability.
2. Roll the right hand wrist on the opening note for a firm, vigorous, but not harsh sound.

Musical Points

1. A fast and happy movement.
2. Avoid a heavy interpretation.
   a. Play repeated notes lightly but not too detached (Measure 10).
      (1) Same technique will be required in the Beethoven *Sonata, Op. 49, No. 2* (Volume 4).

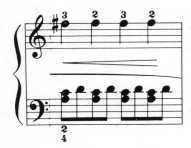

Vivace

Preview

1. Chromatic Scale.
   a. Students enjoy learning this scale, because of the logical fingering.
   b. Strive for fast, secure control. Third finger on black key must be rounded for maximum speed.
   c. Begin preview as soon as student begins to learn the first movement.
   d. For preview, start the student on the scale at middle C and play to the highest key on the piano.

2. Right hand——Measures 32 through 36: Carefully observe fingering.

Technical Points

1. Measure 107 and similar measures are difficult to play hands together.
    a. Counting aloud helps to steady this measure.

2. Last four measures are difficult to play evenly hands together.
    a. Ignore *ff* for the triplet; allow student to play it softly.
    b. Practice slowly in the beginning.

Musical Points

1. Students enjoy the contrasting moods of this fast and happy movement.
   a. The middle section in F major is somewhat slower and very lyrical. (Similar to the "Andante" of the Clementi *Sonatina, Op. 36, No. 1.*)

Theme —— L. van Beethoven

A transcription from *Symphony No. 3* (Eroica).

Preview

1. Measures five and six——Left hand.

Technical Points

1. Techniques much like those in Mozart's *Arietta* from Volume 2.

Musical Points

1. Lovely, serene melody.
2. Most students enjoy making a *crescendo* and *rallentando* simultaneously.

"The Little Rough Rider" from Album for the Young —— R. Schumann

Preview

1. First two measures——Right hand.
   a. Notice——there is no staccato mark over the E in measure two.
      (1) Because note is held, the *sfz* is emphasized.

2. Learn all of right hand to the first double bar.
3. Learn all of left hand from the double bar to the end of that section.
4. Measure 12——Practice hands together.

Technical Points

1. Piece is basically all staccato——a new technique.

Musical Points

1. Students enjoy the image of a wild horseman riding.
2. Has a feeling of continuous motion.
3. Staccato sounds must be crisp and neat.

Ecossaise —— L. van Beethoven

Preview

1. Left hand broken octaves:

2. Measure four——Hands together: Use STOP-PREPARE.

Technical Points

1. First use of the solid octave. (If student cannot reach, play outer note only.)
2. First actual syncopation since *Twinkle Variation B*.

Musical Points

1. Combination of contrasting staccato sounds (*martellato* and light staccato) and contrasting dynamics suggest fun and humor.

Sonatina, Op. 36, No. 3 —— M. Clementi

Spiritoso

Preview

1. Trills (all trills played with same pattern).
   a. Begin preview after student learns *Theme*.
   b. Practice hands together slowly, and gradually increase tempo.

Printed:

Played:

2. Measure seven——Right hand.

3. Measures 42 through 46——Hands together for memory.

Technical Points

This spirited and happy work combines most of the techniques learned so far:

1. Opening technique (like Clementi and Kuhlau sonatinas).
2. Accompaniment pattern in left hand.
3. Rapid scale work.
4. Staccato double thirds.
5. Long trills.

6. Solid octaves.
7. Syncopation.

Musical Points

1. Students love the speed and drama of this sonatina and regard it as a great accomplishment.
   a. Children cannot and should not play rapid passages loudly.
   b. General guide: The faster the playing——the lighter the touch.

Sonatina —— W. A. Mozart

Allegretto

Preview

1. Piece is so difficult that it should be taught section by section in the following way:
   a. Learn right hand first.
   b. Add left hand in segments as each right hand section is perfected.
2. Measures 23 and 24:
   a. Preview when student begins to learn this piece.
   b. Learn hands separately first, then practice hands together.
   c. Use STOP-PREPARE.
   d. Measure 24.
      (1) Right hand must observe tie on A, while other fingers lift at STOP-PREPARE.
      (2) Left hand must lift before rolled chord.

3. Measures 34 through 36——Left-hand pattern varies and is difficult.

4. Measure 48——Right-hand legato fingering is difficult.
   a. Use STOP-PREPARE.
   b. For maximum legato effect, thumb must hold while fifth finger lifts to play next chord.

Technical Points

1. Dotted rhythm must be crisp and consistent throughout the piece.
2. All eighth rests must be observed to keep the rhythmic patterns consistent throughout the piece.
   a. Coordination is difficult when left hand plays during right-hand rests.
   b. Example: Measures 15 and 16——Practice carefully.
      (1) Use STOP-PREPARE for accuracy of hand position: right-hand legato and left-hand lifts.
      (2) Second STOP-PREPARE is for left-hand legato and right-hand lift.

3. New technique: Legato chord motion.
   a. Use STOP-PREPARE.
   b. Right-hand example: Measure 16.

Printed: Played: HOLD 5th
                                    Finger

                                   LIFT
                                   3, 2, 1

c. Left-hand example: Measure 52.

Printed:

                                          Played: HOLD
                                                      2nd Finger
                                                                          etc.

                                                      LIFT
                                                      1 and 5

4. Technically similar to *Arietta* in Volume 2 in many places.

   Musical Points

1. Phrasing, slurring, and rhythm must be meticulous and consistent.
   a. Example: First phrase——Note the *portato* marking for the first note.

2. Rhythm of the G major section suggests a swing. First beats are the forward motion (with emphasis on the dotted eighth note) and the last beats (four, five, and six) are the back swing.
3. C Major section is more dance-like and playful.

Chapter 12
Studying Volume Four

Volume 4 represents the introduction to the mature Classical style. The Mozart *Minuets,* not lengthy but nonetheless major in scope, provide a small taste of the style that will be savored in the sonatas of Volumes 5 and 6. The Beethoven *Sonata* is the bridge between the sonatinas of Volume 3 and the three-movement sonatas of the subsequent volumes. The Bach dance movements mark the culmination of the Baroque style which was introduced in Volume 2 and help to build the facility needed to execute the forthcoming counterpoint.

"Rondo" from Sonatina ——— *W. A. Mozart*

Preview

1. Rolled right-hand chord (Observe second inversion fingering):
   a. Only the high G is *forte,* the preceeding notes are soft.
   b. Left hand plays with low G.

Technical Points

1. Sixteenth notes throughout played softly and evenly.
2. Last two measures: Notice that the right-hand eighth notes are detached.

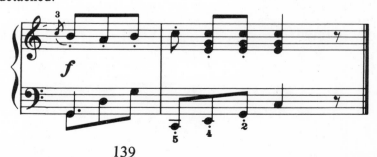

139

3. Measure nine and similar: Left hand. If child cannot span an octave, do not hold the dotted half note.

Musical Points

1. Strive for balance between hands. (Right hand is *f* and left hand is *p*.)
2. First phrase——Right hand
   a. Measure one: the three eighth notes must be detached and even. (Students tend to slur last G to next note.)
   b. Stress the shape of the first phrase.
      (1) Peak of phrase is C.
      (2) Last note of phrase should be played gently, rolling the wrist.

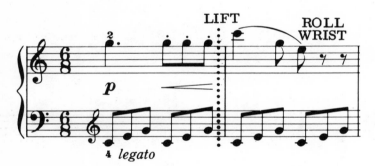

3. An elegant, small-scale rondo.

"Minuet I" from Eight Minuets with Trio, *K315A* —— *W. A. Mozart*

Preview

1. Ornaments:
   a. First trill and similar trills.
      (1) Play softly with no accent.

b. Measure four and similar: Played as follows:

Printed:

c. Measure 26: Trill should be marked as a turn. Play as follows:

Printed:

Corrected:

Played:

Technical Points

1. Measures 14 and 15: The double thirds in the minuet are played slightly detached except where slurred.

Printed:

Played:

2. Left-hand quarter notes played detached throughout.
3. Right-hand quarter notes, unless slurred, played detached in the *Minuet*.
4. In the *Trio,* which contrasts in mood, right-hand notes, although not slurred, are often played legato for the *dolce* effect.

Musical Points

1. *Minuet and Trio* are difficult to play musically, but well worth the effort.
2. Students should be encouraged to enjoy the contrast between the sturdiness of the *Minuet* and the *dolce Trio.*

"Minuet III" from Eight Minuets with Trio *K315A* —— *W. A. Mozart*

Preview

1. Opening double thirds. (Prepare for black keys with hand deep in keyboard.)
   a. Slurring the double thirds *as marked* is a new technique. Lift after first two beats.

Technical Points

1. No new techniques, but difficult to play musically.
2. Measures 27 and 28: Play appoggiatura and quarter note that follows as two even eighth notes.

Musical Points

1. Should have a bright, happy lilt.
2. *Trio* is more lyrical.

"Minuet VIII" from Eight Minuets with Trio *K315A* —— *W. A. Mozart*

Preview

1. Measures five through eight: Octaves.
   a. For children with small hands, play only outer notes.
   b. If played as written, play slightly detached, but light in character.

2. Measures 39 through 42:
   a. Triplets divided between the hands are difficult to play evenly.
   b. Very difficult to jump the interval of a ninth. Use STOP-PREPARE.
   c. Appoggiatura: See example below.
   d. Trill: See example below.

Minuet da Capo

Measure 41:
Played:

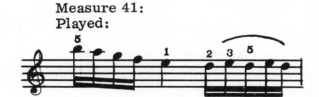

Technical Points

1. Measure two: Play as two even notes, *i.e.*, change grace note to an appoggiatura.

Printed: Played:

2. Triplets divided between hands are a new technique and are a preview for the *Gigue* at end of this volume.

Musical Points

1. Left hand must be light, especially when playing the octaves.
2. *Trio* is lighter in character.
   a. When playing chords, make soprano voice sing above the others.

Musette —— *J. S. Bach*

Preview

1. Measures 13 through 16:
   a. Leaps are awkward. Use STOP-PREPARE.
   b. Syncopation: Feel the accent on the first beat of the left hand.

Technical Points

1. Leaps are difficult. Use STOP-PREPARE.
   a. Example: Opening measures.

Musical Points

1. Opening two-measure statement is playful and delicate, in contrast to the next two measures.

Sonata, Op. 49, No. 2 —— *L. van Beethoven*

Allegro, ma non troppo

Preview

1. First measure plus one beat.
   a. Quality of the opening chord is important; must be solid, but not harsh.
   b. Triplets must be soft, even, and clear.

2. Measure four: Trill. See example below.

Printed:

Played:

3. Measure 12: Turn. See example below.

Printed:

Played:

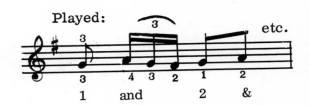

4. Measures 15 through 20: Learn hands separately first.
   a. Left hand is a difficult new technique. It must be played fast, light, and perfectly before attempting hands together.

   b. Right hand must be mastered thoroughly before playing hands together. Do not accent thumb.

   c. Master hands together at tempo.

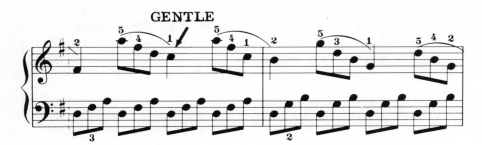

5. Measures 35 and 36: Play grace note ahead of the beat.

   a. Practice measure 35 with STOP-PREPARE.

Technical Points

1. Refer to Henle, Urtext, or Schnabel editions for correct slurrings.

   a. The triplet scale passages in either hand are detached.

      (1) If technique is too difficult, just have student play it as lightly as possible.

      (2) All similar passages should be played lightly in spite of *f* marking.

2. Measures 59 through 62: Play left hand repeated B's as lightly as possible.

3. Measure 109: Trill. See example below.

Printed: Played:

Musical Points

1. Pay careful attention to dynamic markings.
2. Avoid a heavy interpretation, particularly on right-hand repeated notes (see example below). It is believed that this sonata was written earlier than its publication date because it has the character of a sonatina.

3. Most students regard the playing of this piece as a triumph and the teacher should treat it as such.

Tempo di Minuetto

Preview

1. Measures 28 through 34:
   a. Practice hands separately first, then hands together.
   b. Grace note is played before the beat.

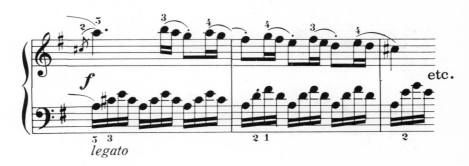

2. Measures 114 to end.
   a. The coordination of hands together is difficult. Practice hands separately first.
   b. Measure 114: Play right hand very lightly and in strict rhythm so that it will not sound like a triplet rhythm.

3. Measures 21 and 22: Coordination of slurs between the hands is difficult.

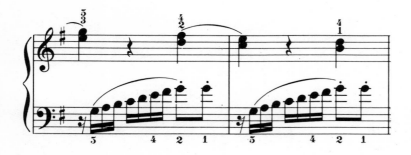

Technical Points

1. Opening rhythms (dotted eighth and 16th notes) must be precise.
   a. Change of finger on the repeated note is essential.

Tempo di Minuetto

2. Measure 68, *etc.*: C Major section.
   a. Refer to Urtext Edition for slurring.
   b. More detached interpretation makes the good humor of this section more apparent.

Musical Points

1. Feeling the swing of the rhythm is the key to musical sensitivity in this movement.
   a. Melodic line and harmonic structure gives illusion of $\frac{6}{8}$ meter. See example below:

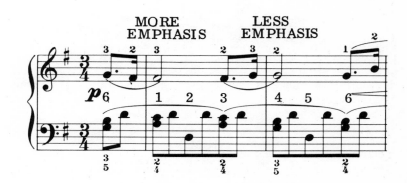

2. Form of this movement is a rondo. Students find it easy to relate
to and remember the order of the sections when we compare the
form of this piece to a layer cake. The theme represents the cake,
the contrasting sections represent the fillings, and the coda (which
begins at measure 107) represents the frosting.

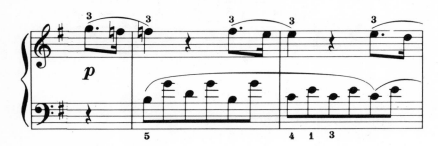

Gavotte in G Minor —— J. S. Bach

Preview

1. Measures 10 and 11: Right hand.
   a. Quarter notes must be legato.
   b. Thumb must be light and detached.
   c. STOP-PREPARE after each thumb note.

2. Measures 24 and 25: Left hand.
   a. Use the same technique as Preview #1 above.

3. Measure 26: We suggest ignoring the finger substitution. Hold thumb
if hand size permits. Note alternate fingering in example:

Technical Points

1. Measure two (last half) and measure three: Note how fourth finger pivots to create legato.

2. Gavotte marks the introduction to three-voice counterpoint. (*Musette* from Volume 3 is two-voice counterpoint with a pedal point.)
   a. Voices must be held for full value (except for small hands).
   b. Fingering is important throughout.
3. Ornament: Trill. See example below:
   a. All ornaments in this piece are executed similarly.

Musical Points

1. Structure of gavotte is rondo form.
2. Phrasing throughout alternates between smooth legato and two-note slurs. This phrasing gives the piece its character.

"Minuet I" from Partita in B Flat —— *J. S. Bach*

An extremely difficult piece. Prepare the student psychologically for spending time learning it; then when good results are achieved, he will be thrilled. If the student has accumulated listening experience and works faithfully, learning will be easier.

Preview

1. Three 16th-note passages: Measures 16, 24, and 38. Play 16th notes softly.

a. Practice hands separately.
b. Practice hands together when each hand is secure alone.
c. Example of 16th-note measure (Measure 24) below:

2. Student must learn and memorize entire piece hands separately.
   a. We suggest two- or four-measure segments at a time.
   b. After dividing the piece into segments, play the Scramble Game to secure memory.

Technical Points

1. Playing the right hand detached is ultimate goal.
   a. Student's playing may take a long time to mature to this point.
2. Left hand is nonlegato throughout, except for the eighth notes (as indicated in the score).
3. Prepare the hand position for black keys by going deeply into keyboard. See example below: Left hand.

Musical Points

1. Wonderful example of two-voice counterpoint which reveals the genius of Bach. Each hand must be secure and independent to achieve both a blending of the two voices and clarity in execution.

"Minuet II" from Partita in B Flat —— J. S. Bach

Preview

None.

Technical Points

1. Learn hands separately in small segments because of difficult voice leading.
   a. Be especially careful with all tied notes.

2. Ornaments:
   a. Measure eight.

Printed:

Played:

   b. Measure 15.

Printed:

Minuet I da Capo

Played:

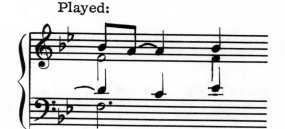

3. Note correct left hand fingering in Measure one.

Musical Points

1. Style is four-voice chorale counterpoint.
2. No pedaling is necessary. Beautiful legato can be achieved with good fingering.
3. Each section repeats as an echo.

"Gigue" from Partita in B Flat —— J. S. Bach

Preview

1. Measures five through eight: Left hand alone.
   a. Ornaments are difficult to fit at tempo.
   b. Play the ornament (*mordant*) on the beat, before the next right-hand note.

Printed:

Played:

2. Measures 25 through 27: Left hand alone for more secure memory (the intervals are difficult).

3. Memorize hands together measure by measure.
   a. Practicing hands together is the only way to make triplets even.

Technical Points

1. Divide the piece into sections for memory.
   a. The Scramble Game is very helpful.
2. Entire piece employs a new and different technique.
   a. Must be learned very slowly because it is extremely difficult.

Musical Points

1. One of the best-loved pieces from Baroque repertoire. Students love to play it well and audiences love to hear it.
2. Numerous interpretive possibilities. We prefer a detached sound in the melody with little or no pedaling.

Chapter 13

Studying Volume Five

Volume Five expands the student's concept of the Classical style by introducing the full three-movement sonata. This concept is the culmination of the progression begun in Volume Two with the sonatina through the two-movement sonata in Volume Four. The two-part Invention and the Prelude from the *Well-Tempered Clavier* expose the student to the standard keyboard works of Bach. The smaller pieces in this volume acquaint the student with the Romantic style, and provide a change from the longer, more complex works.

The *Cuckoo* (Daquin) is postponed until Volume Six, and the Mozart *Sonatas* K545 and K330 are reversed (thus placing K545 in Volume Six). We teach Volume Five in the following order:

1. Für Elise . . . . L. v. Beethoven
2. Arabesque . . . . F. Burgmüller
3. By the Limpid Stream . . . . F. Burgmüller
4. Sonatina in F Major . . . . L. v. Beethoven
5. Old French Song . . . . P. I. Tchaikovsky
6. Prelude . . . . J. S. Bach
7. Invention . . . . J. S. Bach
8. Sonata No. 48, Hob XVI/35 . . . . . . J. Haydn
9. Siciliano . . . . R. Schumann
10. First Loss . . . . R. Schumann
11. Little Prelude . . . . J. S. Bach
12. Sonata K330 . . . . W. A. Mozart

Für Elise —— L. van Beethoven

Preview

1. Measures 12 through 15 (E octaves): Count aloud.

2. Measures 22 through 23: Second ending.
   a. Right hand top Cs are the melody and should be predominant.
   b. Practice left hand carefully.
   c. Hands together: STOP-PREPARE before ornament.
   d. Ornament precedes down beat; fifth fingers play together.
   e. Ornament is soft; melody note (C) is louder.

3. Measures 30 through 34: Practice right hand (forearm rotation) until comfortable when played at tempo.

4. Measures 77 through 82——(a minor arpeggio section): Count aloud.
   a. Phrase carefully; students tend to lift hand instead of rolling thumb under to make a legato arpeggio.

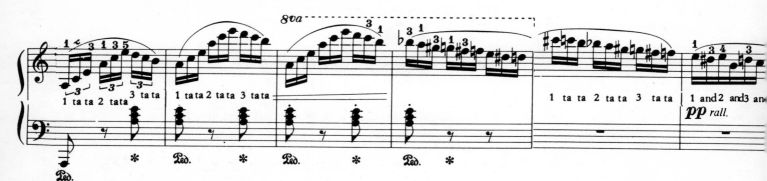

Technical Points

1. Counting aloud greatly facilitates learning of this piece because the problems are caused by the need to fit together the complicated rhythms and fragments which alternate between hands.
2. First piece to require pedal.
3. First piece which has a long series of repeated notes. (Left hand: Measures 60 through 74.)

a. Changing of fingers is essential.
b. Repeated notes must be played softly.

Musical Points

1. Piece can be played expressively without too much rhythmic liberty.
2. Melody should always be played at least *mf* (right hand); left-hand figure is not part of the melody and should be soft.

3. Rapid passages should be played as lightly as possible.

"Arabesque" from Twenty-five Progressive Studies, Op. 100 —— F. Burgmüller

Preview

None. Many students learn this easy piece on their own.

Technical Points

1. Left-hand chords must be soft and light.
2. Keep right-hand fingers rounded for precision.

Musical Points

1. A study for fast, even finger action.

"By the Limpid Stream" from Twenty-five Progressive Studies, Op. 100 —— F. Burgmüller

Preview

1. Right hand first two measures: When thumb plays, wrist drops down and gradually rises while the remaining two notes of the triplet are played, thus returning wrist to a position where it can drop on the next thumb note. This creates a circular motion which keeps the wrist flexible and allows for rapid playing.

Technical Points

1. Right hand must be soft, even, and fast.
2. May be played with the *una corda* pedal.

Musical Points

1. In the first part, melody is always played with the thumb.
2. Left-hand melody in the second part must be legato.

Sonatina in F Major —— L. van Beethoven

Allegro assai

Preview

1. Measures 14 through 17 and 56 through 59.

Measure 14:

Measure 56:

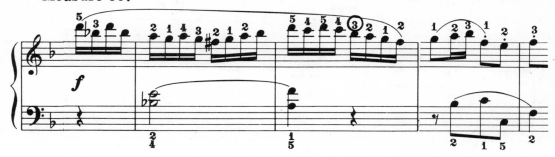

2. First four measures:
   a. Practice hands separately; then hands together.
   b. Coordination of hands together in Measure three is difficult for some.
   c. These measures prepare the student for the character of the entire movement.

3. Measure 21: Coordination of hands together is difficult.
   a. Practice hands together after hands separately is secure.

Technical Points

1. Note slurring in measures nine and ten and 11 and 12.

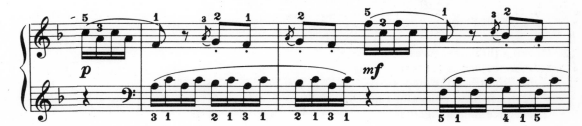

2. Measures 39 through 42: Play smoothly without rushing.

Musical Points

1. This is energetic, happy music.
2. Measures 60 through 63: Right hand asks a question, left hand answers.

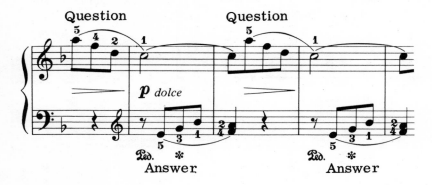

Rondo (Allegro)

Preview

1. Measure four: Turn.
   a. The hand may be lifted to prepare for the turn.
   b. Must be soft, clear, and fast.

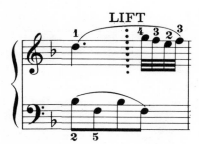

2. Opening three measures:
   a. Practice hands separately first.
      (1) Right hand is staccato.
      (2) Left hand is legato; finger carefully.
   b. Practice hands together.

3. Measure eight: STOP-PREPARE before rolled chord.

4. Measures 21 through 26——Right hand: Accent during practice, to facilitate learning.

   a. Measures 25 and 26——Hands together: Accent left hand for practice.

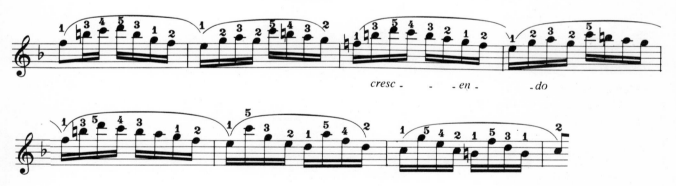

5. Measure 74: Two-note phrases are rapid but retarding, and must join the theme smoothly.

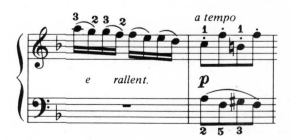

Technical Points

1. Right-hand measures one and two: Sharply contrast the light staccato and the long held-note (roll wrist).

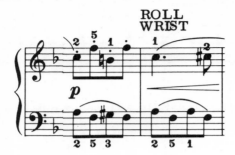

2. Measure 17: Use light staccato.

Musical Points

1. Movement is fast and light.
2. Middle section (d minor) is lyrical.
3. Bring out the imitative beauty of the following:
   a. Measures 49 through 52: Melody in right hand.
   b. Measures 53 through 56: Melody in left hand.

4. Observe graduated dynamics and *tempi*.

"Old French Song" from the **Album for the Young, Op. 39 —— P. I. Tchaikovsky**

Preview

None. After the accomplishments to this point, students find this lovely piece relatively easy to learn.

Technical Points

1. Last two measures (31 and 32): Difficult to bring out the soprano voice against the chords.

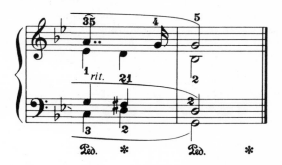

2. Measures 17 through 20: Left-hand staccato passage should not be too heavy.

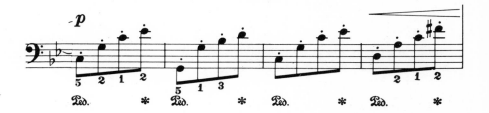

Musical Points

1. Melody must sing.
2. Learn left hand carefully; phrasing and tied notes enhance the feeling of smoothness.

"Prelude in C" from the Well-Tempered Clavier I —— J. S. Bach

Preview

None. Prelude is a series of arpeggiated harmonic progressions. Teach in segments.

Technical Points

1. Must be played evenly; guard against a heavy thumb. Students tend to accent the first right-hand note of each pattern.
2. Left-hand half note must be held (unless the hand is too small).
3. Very difficult to memorize. Divide into sections and use Scramble Game to aid memorization.

Musical Points

1. Dynamics are essential to a musical interpretation. Because there is no rhythmic excitement, no melody, and no form, only the harmony and dynamics give expression.
2. In order to help the students feel the grandeur of this music, we tell them of Bach's great joy in his service to God. During Bach's

lifetime, the Baroque architecture was at its heighth, and some
of the most magnificant cathedrals were built. For many of those
artisans, their contributions to the construction of the cathedrals
were their tribute to God. We draw the analogy that this Prelude
is Bach's musical cathedral, and he builds it little by little until
completion at the climax in measure 30.

Measure 30:

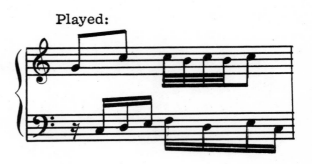

Invention No. 1 in C Major —— J. S. Bach

Preview

None. We teach this in three sections as follows:
Section 1: Measures 1–6.
Section 2: Measures 7–14.
Section 3: Measures 15–22.

Technical Points

1. Ornamentation:
    a. Measure one: Ornament is printed as a *mordant*. We prefer
       a trill. See example below.

Printed:

Played:

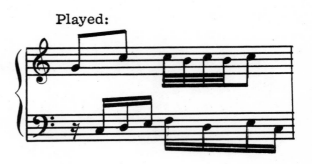

b. Measure two: Ornament is identical to Measure one.

Printed:

Played:

c. Measure five: Play as written (*mordant*).

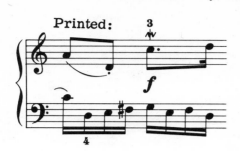

d. Measure six: Play as Measure one:

e. Measure eight: The Bischoff Edition indicates that both autographs show a trill over the F sharp. We enjoy the richness the ornament adds, however, it is clearly optional.

f. Measure 13: Left-hand *mordant*——Play as in Measure five:

g. Measure 14: Trill (like Measure one).

Printed: Played:

h. Measure 20: Griepenkerl autograph has a trill on the fourth
beat over the right-hand E. We enjoy the richness that this
ornament adds; however, it is clearly optional.

Suggested: Played:

2. Counterpoint: Counterpoint of this invention is based on a single
eight-note subject (the first eight notes of the right hand). Subject
occurs 18 times in original form and 19 times in inverted form.
The true art of counterpoint is revealed to the student by the
following multiple uses of the subject:
a. Original subject appears in both the soprano and bass voices
(Measure one).

b. Subject appears in inverted form in measure three of the right
hand and measure nine of the left hand.

Measure 3:   Measure 9:

c. Original subject appears in sequence (Measures 19 and 20).

cresc. *f*

d. Inverted sequence occurs in Measures three and four of the right hand and Measures 11 and 12 of the left hand.

cresc.

e. Measures 15 through 18 alternate both the original and inverted subjects.

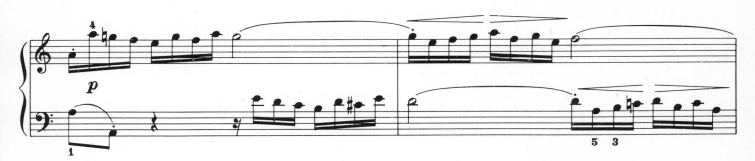

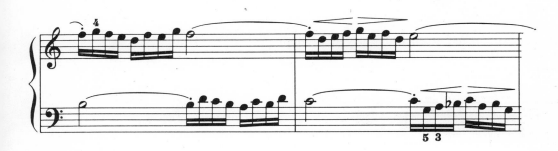

Musical Points

1. Style: Wanda Landowska on the RCA Victor recording (Memorial Edition) calls this invention a Pastorale, a form in literature, art, or music dealing with the subject of shepherds. In music a pastorale is generally associated with the shepherd's flute, and in this invention the thematic material suggests a flute, with the phrasing indicating where a breath must be taken. Inherent serenity and simplicity of the pastoral style suggests a more moderate tempo than the indicated allegro.

2. Phrasing: Subject must be artistically phrased each time it occurs. Staccato markings in the music indicate that the hand must lift (musically suggesting the shepherd's breathing). Since each entry of the subject begins on the second 16th note of a beat, it should be prefaced by a slight lift of the hand.

Sonata No. 48 in C Major, Hob. XVI/35 —— J. Haydn

In Haydn, "the forgotten genius," we find so much more than the kindly old gent of "Papa Haydn" legend. He is the one who bequeathed us the sonata form that Mozart and Beethoven expanded so magnificently; there are no examples in earlier composers of a true parallel to the structure of his symphonies, sonatas, and quartets. But developing the sonata form would be of little consequence if he had not also written music of great beauty, interest, and vitality.

Allegro con brio

Preview

1. Turns: Measure 20 and similar measures.
   a. Practice right hand alone. Practice left hand alone. Then practice hands together as follows:

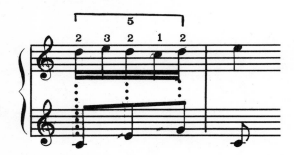

   b. Superimposed rhythm will correct itself when played at tempo. See correct execution below:

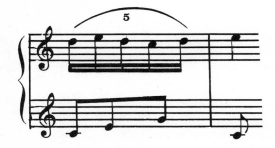

2. Left-hand triplet accompaniment: Measures 20 through 31 (begins with the measure of the first turn).
3. Measure 29 and similar measures: Turn followed by 16th note. Practice hands together as follows:

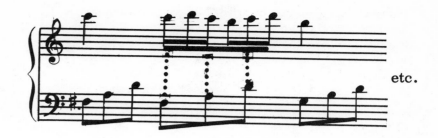

4. Teach first section (to measure 35) hands together.
   a. Secure first section before proceeding to the next.
5. Measures 79 through 100: Practice slowly and carefully.
   a. Children with small hands should play only the lower notes of the octaves (Measures 91 through 93).

Measure 79 etc.

Measures 91–93

Technical Points

1. Measure 10: Three against four; do not try to explain, just demonstrate. Because of the listening, students have no trouble playing this rhythm at tempo.

2. Measures 16 through 19: Note the phrasing in the middle voice.

3. Measures 42 and 43 (and similar passage in recapitulation——
   Measures 132 and 133); For small hands:
   a. Divide the octaves (beginning on the second beat) between two
      hands.
   b. Note suggested fingering.

4. Ornament: Measure 59 trill: Written as an inverted *mordant* in
   the Universal Edition. See example below:

5. Measure 61: Trill written as an inverted mordant in the Universal
   Edition. See example below:

Printed:

Played:

6. Measure 149: Trill——Play as written in following example:

Printed:

Played:

Musical Points

1. Haydn always tried to please both the ordinary music lover and the expert. This movement reveals his craftsmanship and sophistication combined in a work of unfailing good humor and festive spirit. The lightness and merry nature are characterized in the abundant turns and trills.

Adagio

Preview

None. Learn in segments. Few technical problems for a student with established Talent Education background.

Technical Points

1. Ornaments:

   a. Opening rolled chord: Play notes consecutively from bottom to top.

Printed:

Played:

b. Measure three: Trill——See example below:

Printed:

Played:

c. Measure 14: Ornament in the Universal Edition is printed as a turn. See example below:

Printed:

Played:

d. Measure 15: We suggest playing ornament as an unresolved trill. See example below:

Played:

Printed:

e. Measure 16: Resolved trill. See example below:

Printed:

Played:

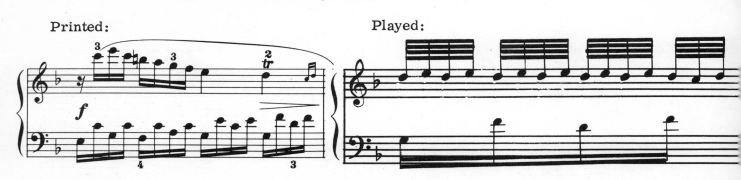

f. Measure 17——Turn. See example below:

Played:

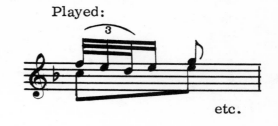

Printed:

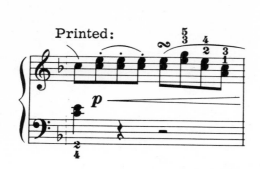

etc.

2. Ornaments after the double bar:
    a. Measure 24——Ornament. See example below:

Printed: Played:

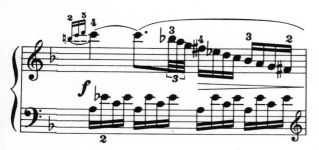   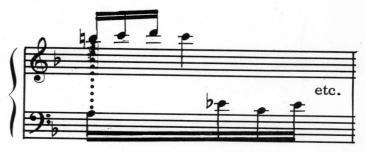

etc.

b. Measure 28——Trill. See example below:

Printed: Played:

   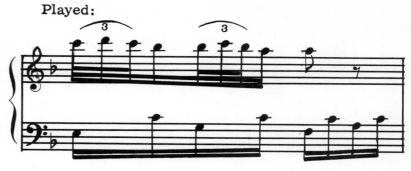

c. Measure 29: Turn. See example below:

Played:

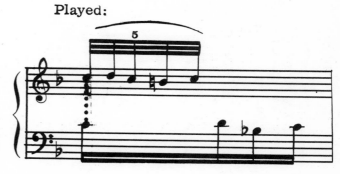

Printed:

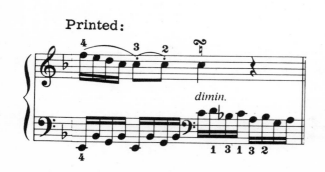

  d. All other ornaments are the same as those in the first half.
3. Note the difference between the left-hand first beats in Measures one and five. (Measure one has an eighth note——Measure five has a quarter note.)

4. Bring out the soprano voice in the double thirds.

Musical Points

1. Interpret as a slow aria. Melody must sing and accompaniment must be played very softly.
2. Movement is in binary form and is the preview for the Scarlatti *Sonata* in Volume 6.

Finale: Allegro

Preview

1. Measures 14 and 16: Left hand is difficult.

2. Measures 30 through 38: Practice hands separately at first. Section is extremely difficult. Preview this passage while the student is memorizing the second movement.

3. Measures 39 through 46: Practice hands separately first.
   a. **PRINTING ERROR:** There are no ties on the first beat in the
      right hand in measures 41 and 44.

4. Measures 54 through 68 (c minor section): Practice hands separately
   first.
   a. Rotary octaves are especially difficult.

   b. Measures 62 and 64: If the hand is small, play G (dotted half
      note) with the left hand.

Technical Points

1. Dotted rhythm must be exact.
2. Be prepared to invest additional time on the middle section (Measures 26 through 68). Entire section is extremely difficult.
3. **PRINTING ERROR:** Remove the first and second ending signs over Measures 53 and 54. (Just before c minor section.)

Musical Points

1. Movement must be rhythmically exciting, light, and crisp.
2. Movement has a form like a minuet and trio. The c minor section sounds mysterious, contrasting the sunny minuet surrounding it.
3. Considering the minuet style, allegro marking should be moderated.

"Siciliano" from Album for the Young, Op. 68 —— R. Schumann

Preview

1. Measures 25 and 26 and measures 29 and 30.
   a. Practice these hands separately first, then hands together.
   b. This section must be fast and light.

Measure 25:

Measure 29:

Technical Points

1. Ornament (Measure 12) is played on the beat.

2. Note the difference between the eighth notes in Measures one and five.
   a. Measure one: *Portato.*
   b. Measure five: Slurred.

3. Slurring, if meticulously observed, is extremely difficult throughout.
4. Play the fast section lightly for speed.

Musical Points

1. First section, which is lilting and playful, contrasts with the driving second section.

"First Loss" from Album for the Young, *Op. 68* —— *R. Schumann*

Preview

1. Left hand——Measures 21 through 25. Observe fingering.

Technical Points

1. Measures 29 and 30: Play eighth notes detached for emphasis.

Musical Points

1. Linger briefly on G's marked *fp* for musical effect.

2. Bring out melodic dialogue between the hands in measures 21 through 25. (See first example for this piece.)

Little Prelude in C Minor ——— J. S. Bach

Preview

None. Prelude is a series of arpeggiated harmonic progressions, like the *Prelude in C Major.*

Technical Points

1. Must be played evenly.
   a. Guard against uneven playing and heavy thumbs, especially on the last two 16th notes of each measure in the right hand.
2. Left hand pattern must be consistent throughout.
   a. Roll wrist on quarter note.
   b. Pattern is Short-Short-Roll (like the opening left hand notes in *Ecossaise* in Volume 2).

3. Difficult to memorize. Divide into sections and play the Scramble Game.

Musical Points

1. Dynamics are the key to musical interpretation.
   a. Climax of entire composition occurs at measure 22.

2. Ends on a dominant chord which reveals Bach's spiritual optimism and perhaps symbolizes hope.

Sonata in C Major, K330 —— W. A. Mozart

Allegro Moderato

Preview

1. Measure two——Trill. See example below:

Printed:

Played:

2. Measures 59 through 63: Hands together.
   a. Note Urtext Edition for phrasing. See example below:

3. Measure 96: Right-hand scale played detached. Difficult at a fast tempo.

4. Measures 129 and 130: See example below:

Printed:

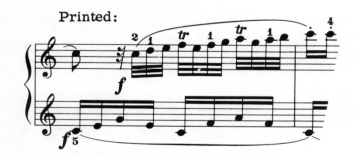

Played:

Technical Points

1. Ornaments:
   a. Measure seven——Trill:

Printed:

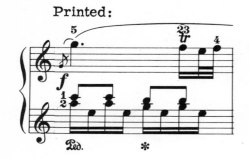

Played:

   b. Measure 17——Right hand——Play 32nd notes evenly:

Printed:

Played:

   c. Measure 19——Two even 16th notes (appoggiaturas, not grace notes, in Urtext Edition):

Printed:

Played:

d. Measure 21——Play grace note as an appoggiatura on the beat with left hand F sharp:

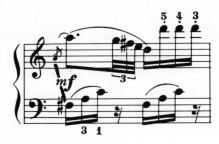

e. Measure 26 and similar measures——Like turns in Haydn *Sonata.* See example below:

f. Measure 27——Appoggiatura played on the beat with left hand C:

g. Measure 37——See example below:

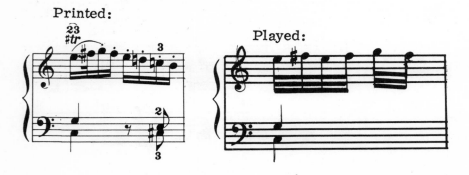

h.   Measure 41——Play two even 16th notes:

Printed:

Played:

i.   Measure 47——See example below:

Printed:

Played:

j.   Measures 54 and 55——See example below:

Printed:

Played:

k.   Measure 65 and similar measures. See example below:

Printed:

Played:

l.   Measure 66 and similar measures——Play three even notes:

Printed:

Played:

m. Measure 78——See example below:

2. Ornamentation in recapitulation (Measure 89 on): The ornaments
   are same as those in the exposition.
3. Check Urtext Edition for phrasing.
4. Measure 18 (and similar measure 105): Play last three left-hand
   16th notes detached.

5. Measure 109——Hands together: Use STOP-PREPARE.

Musical Points

1. Movement has a lovely, spontaneous free style, not adhering to the conventional sonata-allegro form. The three themes of the opening section are related only by their bright quality. The completely independent middle section is clouded by the use of the diminished harmony, and when the recapitulation occurs, the brightness seems even more intense because of the added embellishments.
2. The three opening themes begin as follows:

Measure 5:

Measure 19:

Measure 34:

Andante Cantabile

Preview

1. Measure 13 (Measure 53 is the same): Check Urtext Edition.
   a. In Urtext: Alto voice C is a dotted half note tied to the next measure. B flat is not in Urtext.
   b. Finger substitution is essential.

Suzuki Edition Measure 13:

Urtext Edition Measure 13:

2. Measure 39: Note tied E in right hand lower voice.

3. Measure 11 (Measure 51 is the same).
   a. Note tie in alto of right hand.
   b. Left hand must phrase after the opening chord, while right hand continues phrase.

Technical Points

1. Ornaments:

  a. Measure one and similar measures——Turn. See example below:

Printed:

Played:

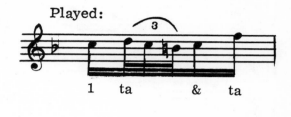

  b. Measures five and six: Play grace note ahead of beat.

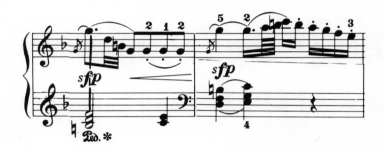

  c. Measure eight and similar measures: Play four even 16th notes:

Printed:

Played:

  d. Measure 15: See example below:

Printed:

Played:

e. Measure 24: Change grace note to appoggiatura and play on the beat with the alto G.

f. Measure 25: Play even 16th notes (grace notes changed to appoggiaturas).

g. Measure 35: Play four even 16th notes.

h. All remaining ornaments are similar to those in first section.
2. Carefully note phrasing as indicated in preview.

Musical Points

1. Movement requires an intimate, expressive interpretation, suggesting the clear and beautiful woodwind sound.
2. Single theme of movement, presented in both major and minor, suggests warmth and coolness.
3. Left-hand accompaniment must be kept very soft, taking special care with the repeated notes in the f minor section.
4. Highlight the left-hand imitation in the contrapuntal part writing in Measures 31 through 34.

Allegretto

Preview

1. Measures nine through 12: Left hand.
   a. Arpeggios and rotary octaves are very difficult.
   b. Note: No slur marking. Play detached if ability permits.

2. Measures 51 and 52 and Measures 55 and 56: Difficult fingering
   pattern in right hand.
   a. Note difference between editions. (Urtext has a B in place
      of the 16th rest.)

Suzuki Edition:
   Measure 51:

   Measure 55:

Urtext Edition:
   Measure 51:

   Measure 55:

3. Measures 124 through 129: Difficult sequence.

4. Measures 166 and 167: Superimposed rhythm (two against three).
   a. New technique.
   b. Teaching aid: Say, "Nice cup of tea."

Technical Points

1. Ornaments:
   a. Measure two and similar measures: Play two even 16th notes.
      (Grace note changed to appoggiatura.)

   b. Measure four and similar: Trill upper note only.

c. Measure 21 and similar: See example below:

d. Measure 33 and similar: Play ahead of beat.

e. Measure 39: Play trill as four even 32nd notes.

f. Measure 60: See example below:

g. Measures 61 and 62: Right hand. Played as Measure 65 is written (triplet).

Measure 61:   Measure 65:

h. Measure 69 and similar. See example below:

Printed: Played:

i.   Recapitulation ornaments are the same as those in the Exposition.
2. Note Urtext Edition for phrasing.
   a. Example: Measures one and two——Left hand is not slurred.
      Play detached.

Urtext Edition

3. Pedal with discretion.
4. Measure 151: Notice the tied C in the tenor voice.

Musical Points

1. Sonata-allegro form.
2. Cheerful movement, whose initial theme has a folk quality, must be played lightly and with good phrasing.

Chapter 14
Studying Volume Six

By the end of Volume Six, the student has experienced the performance of major piano repertoire from all musical periods except contemporary. Prior to Volume Six, experience in the Baroque style has been limited to the study of Bach, now the student is introduced to French (Daquin), German (Handel), and Italian (Scarlatti) styles. With the Mozart *Sonata* K 331, the first experiences in the Classical sonata form are expanded and enriched. Mastering this sonata marks the culmination of the six volumes of study. The Paderewski *Minuet* is in the grand Romantic style and introduces the free-style cadenza, preparing the student for concerto study.

The order of analysis is different from the score listings. We understand from talks with Mrs. Haruko Kataoka that the pieces should be taught in the order listed below, not in the order given in the volumes.

1. Sonata K 545 . . . . W. A. Mozart
2. Sonata "Pastorale" . . . . D. Scarlatti
3. Sonata K 331 . . . . W. A. Mozart
4. The Cuckoo . . . . L. C. Daquin
5. Prelude . . . . G. F. Handel
6. The Harmonious Blacksmith . . . . G. F. Handel
7. Minuet Op. 14, No. 1 . . . . I. J. Paderewski

Sonata in C, K 545 —— W. A. Mozart

This sonata is taught after Mozart Sonata in C, K 330 (Volume Six). It contains the rudiments that Mozart expected a student beginning piano study to learn. Mozart, like Bach, had high standards. After the student has mastered the Mozart Sonata K 330, this sonata will be relatively easy.

Allegro

Preview

1. Measure 11——Left hand alone at first; then hands together.
   a. If pedal is used, avoid over-pedaling. We prefer it without.

Measure 11:

2. Measure 25——Trill: Hands together.
   a. Play a measured trill——count aloud.
   b. Student should practice slowly at first.

Printed:

Played:

3. Measures 50 through 53: Left hand fingering extremely important. See example below.

Technical Points

1. Note Urtext Edition for slurring.
2. Scale and arpeggio passages should be played as lightly and detached as possible. The convention in Classical music is that unless specifically slurred, all notes are played detached.
3. Trills and ornaments.
   a. Measure 4.

Played:

etc.

   b. Measures 15 and 17.

Printed:

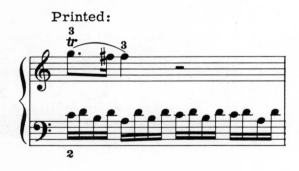

Played:

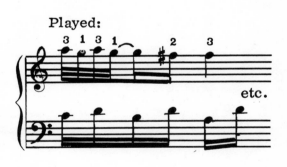

etc.

   c. Measure 22———Grace notes played ahead of the beat.

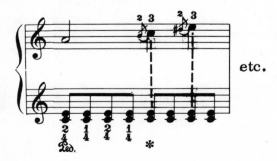

etc.

　　　d. All remaining ornaments are identical to those in the exposition.
4. Carefully observe fingerings.
　　　a. We do not change fingers in Measures 13 and 22 and similar
　　　　measures.

Measure 13:

Finger 2-1 throughout this measure.

Measure 22:

Finger 2-4 throughout.

Musical Points

1. Play left hand Alberti bass patterns and accompaniments softly.
2. Play all rapid passages lightly and evenly.
　　　a. Avoid a heavy sound on the thumb notes.
3. Avoid excessive pedaling.

Andante

This movement illustrates Mozart's resourceful use of the Alberti figuration.

Preview

1. Left hand——Measures 20 through 24. An unusual and intricate Alberti figuration.

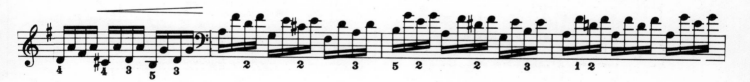

Technical Points

1. Observe Urtext Edition phrasing and slurring.
2. Technically not difficult to execute, but extremely difficult to memorize.
　　　a. Learn slowly and carefully, one segment at a time.

Musical Points

1. Homophonic style throughout movement.
　　　a. Right hand must sing.
　　　b. Left hand played *pp* throughout.
2. Beautiful phrasing and shaping are essential.

Rondo (Allegretto)

Preview

1. First four measures: Basis of piece.
   a. Most desirable to bring out upper voice in the double thirds.
   b. Difficult to play and should be previewed while the student is memorizing the second movement.

2. Right hand——Measures 14 and 15: Awkward leap from fourth to second finger.

3. Measures 30 through 39: Difficult hands together.

4. Measures 60 through 64: Difficult hands together.

5. Measure 69: Correct fingering is crucial.

Measure 69:

Technical Points

1. Refer to Urtext Edition for slurring and staccato.
2. Measure 10——Use STOP-PREPARE.

3. Measure 35——Phrase between D sharp and High C.

4. Measure 71 to end.
   a. Left-hand eighth notes must be firmly played.
   b. STOP-PREPARE after last 16th note of measure for accuracy of left-hand octave.

Measure 71:   STOP-PREPARE

Musical Points

1. Upper voice in the double thirds must be prominent.
2. Interpretation should be light, happy, and clear.
3. Note right-hand and left-hand imitation.
   a. Keep left hand softer in these passages. (Bass piano strings are heavier.)

Sonata "Pastorale," L. 413 —— D. Scarlatti

In the more than 500 *Essercisi* which Scarlatti wrote for the keyboard (incorrectly labeled sonatas), he used a small-scale plan of composition known as binary form. In this pastorale, we hear the shepherd's flute melody (pastorale), accompanied intermittently by the plucking of guitars.

Preview

1. Measure 17: Trill with a held note——a new technique.

Printed:

Played:

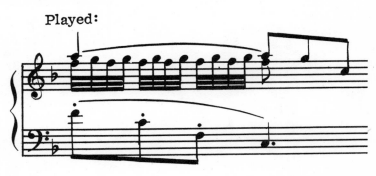

2. Measures 8 through 10 and 43 through 45: Parallel scales in thirds.
   a. New technique.
   b. Carefully observe fingerings.
   c. Balance to upper voice is important.

Printed:

Technical Points

1. Ornaments: Must be fast and light.
   a. Measure 2: Trill——Four notes per beat beginning on the upper auxiliary.

Played:

etc.

b. Measure 12: Trill——Four notes per beat beginning on the main note G——*not* the auxiliary as written.

Printed:

(313)

Played:

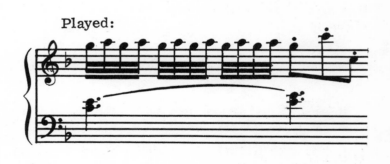

c. All other trills: Play four notes per beat beginning on the indicated note.

Musical Points

1. Interpretation: Gentle pastoral feeling. Do not be unduly influenced by the *Allegro* indication.

Sonata in A Major, K331 —— *W. A. Mozart*

Mozart has often been called the first important virtuoso pianist and his understanding of the keyboard is unsurpassed. That understanding, combined with his genius in creating works of incomparable unity, has given us this powerfully affective *Sonata* in A major. Each movement of this *Sonata* can, and often does, stand alone; however, Mozart unites the movements, creating an organic whole, by the use of thematic foreshadowing between Variation VI and the Alla turca and between Variation IV and the Trio.

It is one of the best-loved pieces in the Classical literature and rightly so because it combines melodic beauty, rhythmic vitality, and a perfect organization of thematic material.

Andante grazioso

This movement is in the form of a theme and variations and could easily stand alone. Each phrase is intensely expressive, and combines perfectly with the others to create this masterpiece.

Theme

Preview

None. Teach phrase by phrase.

Technical Points

1. Ornament (Measure 10): Play before the beat for a more pleasing musical effect.

2. Measure 17——Last beat: Play right hand carefully without rushing to the first beat of next bar.

Musical Points

1. Melody in upper voice must sing throughout.
2. Careful pedaling required for beautiful phrasing.
3. Measures 11–12: Great care is needed for *sf* markings, slurs, and staccato. The *sf* markings suggest subtle emphasis rather than strong accent.

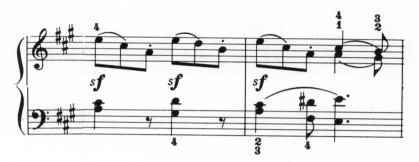

Variation I

Preview

None. Teach phrase by phrase.

Technical Points

1. Trill——Measure 25.

2. Measure 35, last beat to first beat of measure 36: Do not rush the octave leap. Use pedal to avoid breaking phrase.

Musical Points

1. Phrase opening figure carefully.
   a. Right hand must float off for rests to avoid a percussive effect.
   b. Left hand should be played softly and caressingly and may be pedaled discretely. Urtext Edition does not have left hand marked staccato.

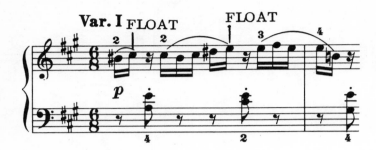

2. Measure 23: Do not take the *forte* marking too seriously; it should become richer in quality, rather than rough and heavy.

3. Measures 28–29.
   a. The *sf* markings are suggestions of emphasis rather than accent. Remember these are within the context of a *p* dynamic marking.
   b. Portato notes may be played with pedal to avoid excessive emphasis.

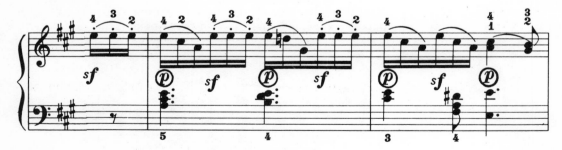

Variation II

Preview

1. Measures 41 and 42——Last beat in each.

a. Note suggested alternate fingerings.
b. Awkward until well-practiced.

Technical Points

1. Ornaments.
    a. Measure 37 and all others (except measures 45 and 46).
        (1) Comparable to turns in the Haydn Sonata, first movement
             (Measure 20) in Volume Five.

Printed:

Played:

        (2) Ornament may be practiced slowly as follows. Rhythm will
             correct itself when played at tempo.

b. Trill——Measures 45 and 46: Play as written in example.

c. Left hand grace notes: Play before the beat——quick and light.

2. Measure 37, last beat and similar measures: Four against three (superimposed rhythm).
    a. Similar to Haydn Sonata, first movement (Measure 10) in Volume Five.

Musical Points

1. All trills must be played clearly and lightly.
2. Left-hand triplets must be even and soft.
3. Note the large dynamic contrasts which give character to this variation.

Variation III——Minore

Preview

1. Octave passages (Measures 59 through 62).
   a. Practice right-hand thumb alone for soft, even sound of alto line.
   b. Careful pedaling required for legato effect.

etc.

   c. For children who cannot span an octave, play upper note only.
2. Measure 65 (second half)——Left-hand double thirds: Alternate fingering:

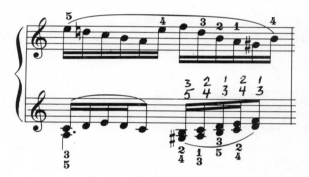

Technical Points

1. Ornament in Measure 66: Play as noted.

Printed: Played:

Musical Points

1. Style and mood are very romantic.
2. Play octaves as smoothly as possible.
3. Measures 71 and 72: Note intensity increasing to the end of the Variation creating a fine contrast to the opening of Variation IV.

Begin *mf* and grow to *f* .

Variation IV

Preview

1. Opening Measures 73 through 76: Cross-over of hands.
   a. Hand crossing is the main technique of this variation.

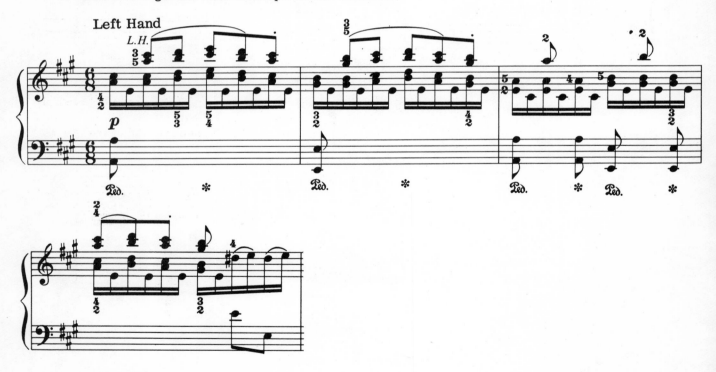

Technical Points

1. Measures 80 and 90: Alto voice is not marked staccato in the Urtext Edition. Play smoothly.

Suzuki Edition:

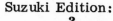

Urtext Edition:

2. Measure 73 and similar passages: Phrasing slurs over all of left-hand soprano double thirds in Urtext Edition.

Suzuki Edition:

Urtext Edition:

Musical Points

1. Variation suggests softly ringing chimes surrounding beautiful soprano melody in beginning of second part.
2. The *sf* marking in measure 83 suggests emphasis rather than strong accent.

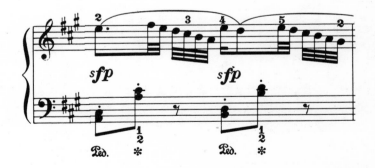

Variation V——Adagio

Careful listening to the recording eliminates problems with complicated rhythms.

Most difficult Variation to learn and memorize.

Preview

1. Measure 100: Complicated rhythmic pattern. Must be secure hands separately. Then practice hands together.

2. Measure 107: Combination of phrasing and rhythm is difficult.

3. Especially important to learn this variation phrase by phrase.

Technical Points

1. Ornaments: Play as noted.
   a. Measure 103: Pay special attention to correct execution in footnote.

Printed:

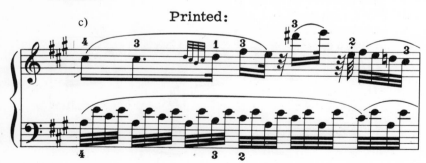

Play:

Played:

2. Repeated notes must be executed gently (Measure 97 and similar measures).
   a. Note: Ornament at beginning of Measure 97 is not in Urtext Edition.

Urtext Edition:

(lightly)

Musical Points

1. Variation embodies a wide variety of pianistic techniques which, when mastered, exemplify Mozart's great genius. These include:
   a. Singing melodic line.
   b. Florid passages.
   c. Double third passages.
   d. Staccato runs.
   e. Repeated notes.
   f. Ornaments.
   g. Complicated rhythms.
2. Allow time for the interpretation of this variation to mature.

Variation VI——Allegro

Preview

1. Measures 113 through 116.
   a. Master the right hand first.
   b. Left hand——Rolled chords.
      (1) First chord in each measure is emphasized; the second chord is light.
      (2) Roll chords quickly.
   c. Left hand——Practice eighth notes.
   d. Practice these measures hands together.

Measure 113:

2. Measure 120: Left-hand rolled chords——difficult to play at tempo.

3. Measures 125 and 126: Practice hands separately, then hands together.

Technical Points

1. Rapid passages must be executed clearly.
2. Measures 138 through 140: The 16th note preceeding the ornament is treated as part of the ornament.

Musical Points

1. Variation is a happy finale which not only concludes first movement, but also foreshadows the third movement, *alla Turca.* (Measures 117–120).

Minuet

A dance, and in spite of Mozart's ingenious phrase construction, the rhythm must flow smoothly.

Preview

1. Measure 12: Play the repeated F sharps carefully; they add much to the beauty of this line. (Compare similar passage at Measure 44.)

2. Measures 30 and 31: Use STOP-PREPARE.

3. Learn remainder of movement carefully in segments.

   Technical Points

1. Measure one: In spite of Classical tradition which suggests that ornament be played on the beat, it is musically more satisfying when played ahead of beat.

2. Measure 11: Ornament is similar to measure one: Play ahead of the beat.

3. Grace notes (Measures 17, 19, and 47): Play quickly ahead of beat.

Measure 17:   **Measure 19:**   **Measure 47:**

4. Ornament (Measure 40): Play as noted.

Printed: Footnote: Played:

  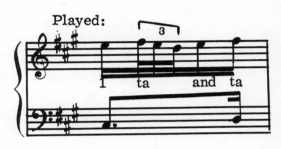

5. Trill (Measure 47): Play as follows:

Printed: Played:

6. Measures 20, 21, and 22: Right-hand 16th note at end of measure should not be a short staccato. Play either attached or *portato*.

Measure 20:

cresc.

Musical Points

1. Melody with accompaniment.
   a. Play left hand softly throughout.
   b. Left hand octaves, in particular, must be played so that they do not overpower melody.
2. All ornaments are played lightly.
3. Dynamics are clearly marked and must be observed carefully.
   a. The *sfp* marking (Measure 29) is not in Urtext Edition. May be thought of as suggesting emphasis since it is the climax of phrase.

Trio

Note the similarity of construction between the Trio and Variation IV. Reveals Mozart's genius in unifying entire Sonata.

Preview

An extremely difficult movement. Be prepared to spend enough time for student to become comfortable with the crossing of hands.

1. Measure 50: Double thirds fingering is a new technique. STOP-PREPARE for pivoting on fourth finger (E) to 3/1 on F sharp/D.

Printed:

Played:

2. Measure 54: Right-hand double sixths. Fingering plus holding of essential notes allows this to be played legato. In similar situations, hold down nonrepeated finger while lifting the finger that has to play the next note.

Printed:

Played:

3. Measures 56 through 58: Practice hands together. Treat ornaments as grace notes, play ahead of beat.

Urtext Edition:

Technical Points

1. Student must be secure with difficult right hand in each hand-crossing section before being allowed to play hands together.
2. Precise fingering is essential.
   a. Measures 52 and 53: Right hand as inner voice. Note alternate fingering. We prefer Urtext Edition fingering.

Suzuki Edition:

Urtext Edition:

   b. Measure 60: Note alternate fingering for right hand. We prefer Urtext Edition fingering.

Suzuki Edition:

Urtext Edition:

3. Octave passage (Measures 68 through 72).
   a. Do not play too heavily, even though marked *f*.
   b. Use portato rather than staccato touch.

c. Students with small hands, play outer notes only.

4. Learn in segments for best results.
5. To ease execution of left hand crossings, have student count aloud. Counting seems to give a psychological expansion of time so that the student does not feel rushed into moving the hand over and finding the new note accurately.

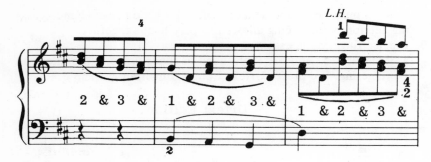

Musical Points

1. Interpretively, cross-over of hands doubles the upper right-hand voice and creates the effect of chimes.
2. Melodies heard in middle register seem like a question which is immediately answered in the upper voice.

alla Turca——Allegretto

Opening of *alla Turca,* consisting of melodic fragments, creates a momentum which builds and subsides throughout the movement while increasing in intensity to its dramatic conclusion.

Preview

1. Measure nine: Crossing over double third at a fast tempo is difficult. Use STOP-PREPARE.

2. Measures 26 through 32: Left-hand rolled chords. Procedure for practicing:
   a. Measures 28 and 29.
      (1) Play as solid chords.
      (2) STOP-PREPARE before each.
      (3) Hand position moves deep into keyboard for D sharp chord and moves back out for E chord.
      (4) Practice as written (Rolled).
   b. Practice entire passage——Left hand alone.
   c. Practice passage hands together with STOP-PREPARE.
      (1) Because of tempo, rolled notes are played before the beat.

3. Measures 32 through 41: Intricate right-hand fingering requires careful practice. (Note suggested alternate fingering.)

Suzuki Edition:

Urtext Edition: Alternate Fingerings

4. Rotary octaves (Measures 89 through 95): Very difficult!
   a. Practice right hand. STOP-PREPARE between octaves.
   b. Most difficult are the octaves on the black keys.
      (1) Helpful mental image for students is to think of anchoring the fifth finger on the black key before moving to the next thumb note.
   c. Practice hands together using STOP-PREPARE before each left-hand rolled chord.

5. Coda.
   a. Right-hand chords (Measure 97 and 98).
      (1) Small hand may play only three upper notes.
      (2) Chord is not rolled in the Urtext Edition. We recommend Urtext.
      (3) When played hands together, roll left-hand notes before beat.

Suzuki Edition:

Urtext Edition:

   b. Measures 99 and 100: Right-hand phrasing is difficult. Practice carefully and STOP-PREPARE before chord.

   c. Measure 101——Grace-note chords: Difficult to play at tempo unless thought of as being *almost* a solid four-note chord.

   d. Right-hand ornament (Measure 109 through 111): Less difficult alone, but very difficult when played with left hand. STOP-PREPARE before each one.

e. Measures 115 and 116: STOP-PREPARE before chord.

f. Measures 121 and 122: Note difference in Urtext Edition of chord in Measure 122. We use Urtext version (with suggested fingering) which greatly facilitates playing first beat and following octave.

Suzuki Edition: **Urtext Edition:**

Technical Points

1. Fingering should be observed carefully.
   a. Give attention to placement of thumb in opening measures and similar passages.

b. Measures 20 through 23 left hand: Note suggested fingerings.

c. Measures 41 through 47: STOP-PREPARE at repeated notes.

2. Ornaments.
   a. Measures five through seven: STOP-PREPARE before ornament.

b. Trill (Measure 23): Play as written below:

Printed:

Played:

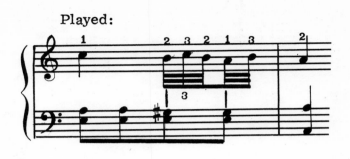

3. Most technical points in movement are covered in preview.

Musical Points

1. Contrasting textures of sounds (octaves, rolled chords, and 16th-note passages) build momentum and give movement its unique character.
2. Following section (Measures 32 through 41) was foreshadowed in Variation VI of first movement.

3. Tempo marking is only *allegretto*. Unnecessary to play faster although some performers do play it faster.
4. Coda is a grand flourish and must drive forward to last chord.

The Cuckoo —— L. C. Daquin

This delightful piece sounds easy and brilliant, but in fact, is extremely difficult to play well. May be taught in sections. Previews represent the most difficult parts in the entire piece.

Preview

1. Measures five through nine: Right hand.
   a. Passage is basis of piece and must be played perfectly.
   b. Use fingering marked. STOP-PREPARE between sequence repetitions.

2. Opening three measures: Teach fourth-finger precision. This technique is typical of the rapid, light, precise Baroque style of keyboard playing. Preview right hand.

3. B minor section (Measures 84 through 86): Needs practice because of thumb on black key.

4. E major section——Right hand.
   a. Measures 66 through 69: Inversion of opening pattern.

   b. Measures 74 through 79: Technically difficult because fifth finger
      must reach for black key.

   Technical Points

1. Piece requires strong fingers, flexible wrists, and a relaxed upper
   arm.
2. Ornaments:
   a. Measure four and all similar ornaments.
      (1) STOP-PREPARE before inverted mordant. (May lift to
          prepare.)
      (2) Play mordant on the beat——fast, lightly and clearly.

   b. Measures 10 and 11: Use STOP-PREPARE before ornaments.
      (1) Measure 11: Play all four notes with the left hand B (first
          note).
      (2) Play all similar ornaments the same way.

c. Measure 22: Needs a rich trill because of *ritardando*. (See example below):

Printed:

Played:

(1) Measure 41——G major section: Similar trill.
d. Measure 82——Trill: Begin on upper auxiliary. See example below:

Printed:

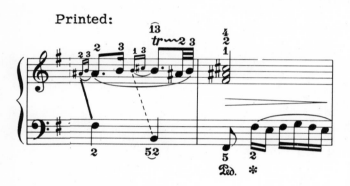

Played:

3. Left hand——Measure 11: STOP-PREPARE after first note (B). Play remaining notes fast, evenly, lightly, and clearly.

Musical Points

1. Cuckoo sound, like the bird's true call, should be delicate.
   a. Right hand predominates with melody at least at a *mf* dynamic level, otherwise, the left hand passages sound awkward or too heavy.
2. Good example of rondo form.

3. Climax of piece occurs in Measure 79. See example below:

Prelude —— G. F. Handel

Preview

1. Finger substitution.
   a. Practice first measure hands together, using STOP-PREPARE to perfect finger substitution.
   b. Finger substitution occurs almost simultaneously with left-hand fifth finger note.

2. Entire piece may be learned hands together.

Technical Points

1. Ornaments in the first half:
   a. Measure six——Right-hand trill: See example below:

Printed:

Played:

b. Measure 10——Right-hand trill. See example below:

Printed: Played:

c. Measure 11 and similar ornaments: Play as a mordant ahead of beat. Use STOP-PREPARE to lift hand ahead of ornament.

STOP-   STOP-
PREPARE   PREPARE

d. Measure 13——Right-hand trill: See example for Measure 11.
2. Ornamentation in second half: All ornaments are parallel to examples in first half.

   Musical Points

1. Prelude is in simple binary form (like the Scarlatti sonata, but easier).
2. We prefer a clear, unpedaled (or very discretely pedaled) interpretation.
3. Graduated dynamics of sequences create the charming character of piece.

"The Harmonious Blacksmith" from Suite in E, No. 5 —— G. F. Handel

This Air and variations does not sound complicated, but the many small details that make this piece exciting require careful attention in order to create the Baroque style. In its original form, it is called Air and doubles, meaning just that: each variation seems to double or become faster when in actuality, Handel cleverly uses more notes per beat while maintaining a constant underlying beat. He begins the Air with eighth notes, then uses 16th notes in the right hand in Variation I, 16th notes in the left hand in Variation II, 16th-note triplets in the right hand in Variation III, 16th-note triplets in the left hand in Variation IV, and 32nd notes in Variation V.

Air

Preview

None. Learn carefully phrase by phrase working hands separately at first.

Technical Points

1. Pay close attention to length of notes in lower three voices. (Rests and ties must be scrupulously observed for maximum beauty.)
   a. Must be learned carefully hands separately.
2. Measure five: Note correction in slur and fingering.

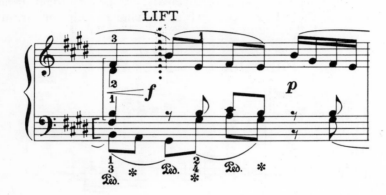

3. Pedal carefully to avoid smudging sounds.

Musical Points

1. Bring out soprano voice of this four-voice chorale-like theme.
2. Careful phrasing is essential.

Variation I (Un poco piu animato)

Preview

1. Left Hand——Measures one and two: Observe fingering, ties, and length of notes.

Technical Points

1. Beware of heavy thumb in right-hand nonmelody notes.
   a. Example: Measure one——Right hand——melody must be prominent.

(1) — symbolizes emphasis and ⌣ symbolizes lightness.

etc.

2. Measures six and seven: Right hand plays tenor notes.

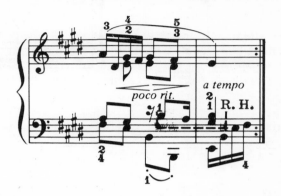

Musical Points

1. Bring out theme, while enjoying feeling of increased motion.
2. Pedal discretely.

Variation II (Più mosso)

Preview

1. Left-hand ornament——Measures seven and eight.
   a. Mordant with a prefix (Vorschlag).
   b. See example below for execution.
   c. STOP-PREPARE after D sharp preceeding ornament.
      (1) Slight lift of hand is helpful after playing the D sharp to
          execute ornament with clarity.

Printed:

Played:

STOP-
PREPARE

Technical Points

1. Ornament (Trill)——Measures five and six——Right hand: See
   example below:

2. Learn first-section right hand carefully, observing tied notes in
   soprano.

non legato leggiero

Musical Points

1. Left hand must be detached and very light.
2. We suggest that dynamics follow the general shape of the Air.

Variation III (Vivace)

Preview

1. Measures five and six: Right hand.
   a. Playing the fourth finger in measure six seems uncomfortable
      until practiced well.

Technical Points

1. Carefully note fingering.
2. Left hand: observe note values and rests.
   a. Staccato markings are editorial and should be played detached, but not too short.

Musical Points

1. *Sempre legato* marking suggests a rich sound. We prefer a light, crisp interpretation.

Variation IV (L'istesso Tempo)

Preview

1. Entire left hand (Fingering is difficult).
   a. Note suggested alternate fingerings.
2. Right hand——Measures three through six: Tied notes and fingering are very difficult.

Technical Points

1. Left hand must be played lightly and clearly.
2. Right hand tied notes are difficult. Practice entire right hand separately.
3. Practice hands together in segments. This is the most difficult variation.

Musical Points

1. Rapidly moving left hand must not overpower melodic beauty of theme which appears in both alto and soprano voices.

Variation V (Vivacissimo)

Preview

None. If student can play E major scale, he can play this Variation; if not, preview E major scale.

Technical Points

1. Rapid scale passages: observe accents and fingerings.
   a. Note alternate fingering in right hand——Measure nine.

2. Observe voice-leading in left hand in preceeding example (Similar to measures five and six).

Musical Points

1. Variation must be played rapidly, but never out of control. It is the vigorous culmination of this masterpiece.

Minuet Op. 14, No. 1 —— I. J. Paderewski

This is the most romantic piece in the Suzuki piano repertoire. Students enjoy the warmth and expressive qualities of the music. It should be regarded as a delightful prelude to their future study of the Romantic literature.

Preview

1. Measures 29 through 32——Right-hand scale passage and cadenza.

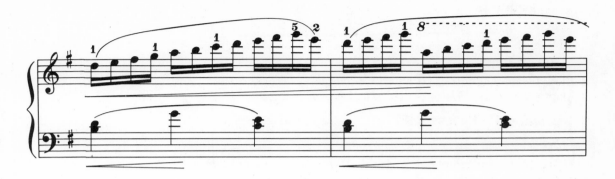

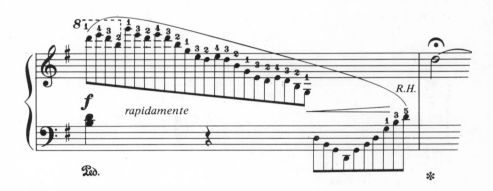

a. Following fingering, divided between the hands, is easier and may be used at teacher's discretion.

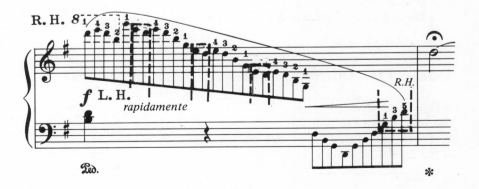

2. Measures 61 through 68: Long trill.
   a. Practice slowly playing four sixteenth notes per beat. See below.

 Printed:

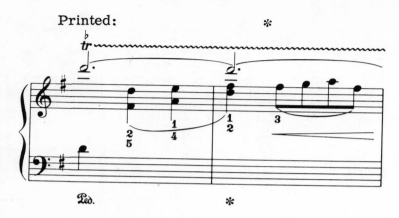

Played:

3. Measures 69 and 70: Do not attempt this passage hands together until student can play above trill rapidly.
   a. When trill is automatic, student should concentrate on left-hand notes, listening particularly for ornament.

Printed:

Played: etc.

4. Trills in Coda——Measures 113 through 116. See example below:

Printed:

Played:

5. Measures 131 and 132——Hands together: Arpeggio.
   a. Practice well hands separately first.

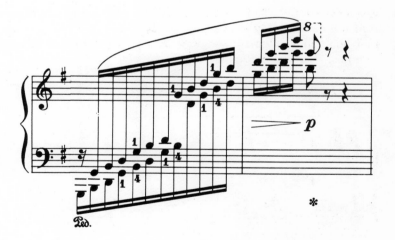

Technical Points

1. Opening *non legato* should not be taken too literally. Discrete pedaling is permissable.

2. Ornaments:
    a. Opening turn——Measure one:

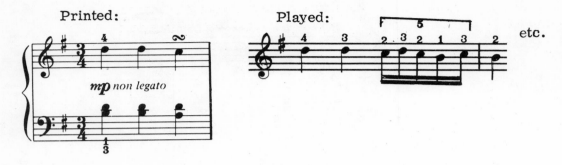

    b. Measure five: Ornament may be counted as follows:

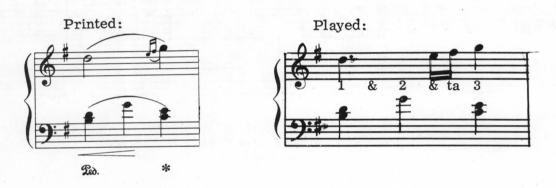

    c. Measures eight and nine: STOP-PREPARE for grace notes.

    d. Measures 44, 48, and similar measures: ornaments may be thought of as last half of the preceding beat.

Printed:

Played:

e. Measure 49: *sf* on low G so that tone lasts for entire passage; play melody in upper voice softly.

3. Measures 21 through 23: Practice left-hand parallel octaves carefully.

4. Measures 117 through 130: Practice right hand alone, observing
   fingering carefully.

Musical Points

1. Careful listening to a fine interpretation will assist the student
   enormously!
2. Opening theme must feel like a dance. Over-pedaling will detract
   from iilting feeling.

3. Enjoy dramatic crescendos in octave passages, but exercise great care so that octaves do not overpower the right hand.
4. Section marked "con forza la melodia" must sing like a little lament, building to long trill and then fading into a return of the theme played *pianissimo*.
5. Coda begins delicately and contains an exciting *accelerando* which pushes the piece to bottom of keyboard, and then allows pianist to float to top and end gently.

Bibliography

Axline, Virginia M. *Dibs in Search of Self*. New York: Ballantine, 1964.

Briggs, Dorothy Corkille. *Your Child's Self Esteem*. New York: Doubleday & Company, Inc. 1975.

Doman, Glenn. *How To Teach Your Baby to Read*. New York: Random House, 1964.

Dyer, Wayne W. *Your Erroneous Zones*. New York: Funk & Wagnalls, 1976.

Ginott, Haim. *Between Parent and Child*. New York: The Macmillan Company, 1965.

Ginott, Haim G. *Between Parent and Teenager*. New York: The Macmillan Company, 1969.

Ginott, Haim G. *Teacher and Child*. New York: The Macmillan Company, 1972.

Gordon, Thomas. *Parent Effectiveness Training*. New York: Peter H. Wyden, Inc., 1970.

Gordon, Thomas. *Teacher Effectiveness Training*. New York: David McKay Company, Inc., 1974.

Honda, Masaaki. *Suzuki Changed My Life*. Evanston, Illinois: Summy-Birchard Company, 1976.

Mills, Elizabeth and Murphy, Sister Therese Cecile. *The Suzuki Concept*. Berkeley, California: Diablo Press, Inc., 1973.

Suzuki, Shinichi. *Nurtured By Love*. Jerico, New York: Exposition Press, Inc., 1969.

Appendix I

Index of Pieces

244

Appendix II

Index of Composers